Color Me
CANINE

A coloring book for dog lovers of all ages!

by

SANDY BERGSTROM MESMER

Sandy Bergstrom Mesmer Designs
Clearwater, FL
2021

Table of Contents

Forward

July 2021

Welcome to "Color Me Canine (Hound Group)".

Every once and a while it can be fun to imagine an Ibizan Hound bright blue. Or a Dachshund with red and white stripes.

As crazy as it may seem, it can be super relaxing to color a Portuguese Podengo Pequeno bright red and purple.

It lets us cut loose. As breeders we put all our attention on preserving our breeds. We sweat each detail, making sure that each generation is as good as they can possibly be. We want everything to be PERFECT, exactly according to the standard.

In this volume, you can let your imagination go bonkers.

As I wrote each description I'd say to myself, oh, I'd love having a dog that intuits my every mood (Irish Wolfhound). Or I'd love a dog that one expert described as living with "a circus of flying monkeys" (Petit Basset Griffon Vendeen). Really, I would. I would probably just sit and stare at my stunning Redbone Coonhound. And who can say no to a piece of history like the English Foxhound?

Obviously, I'm not going to get all these dogs – for one thing my own dogs would move out. But I can celebrate them, just like I celebrate every wonderful dog breed out there.

This book is dedicated to all the breeders who helped me understand their hounds. Kerrie Kuper, Caroline Coile, Jean Evanoff, Mia Speciale, Dan Stolz, Alan Reznik, Anthony Clemento and Sam Taylor, just to name a few. Thank you!

Sandy Bergstrom Mesmer

The Partnership with a Hound

I think the frustration with hounds comes from a lack of understanding of them and what their original purpose for being selectively bred.

Hounds do not believe that they NEED you. You are a lovely part of their day - like a favorite coffee cup or a favorite pair of shoes. If the cup is broken or the shoes are lost, we can get along just fine with another. Let me explain:

Where other breeds of dogs like Labradors, Shepherds, Border Collies, and a host of others are bred to work WITH man; their original bred temperament is to work alongside man in cooperation to achieve a goal.

The Border Collie follows man's commands to herd the livestock. The Lab follows the hunter's commands to get the quarry - so and so forth. They are a teammates of man. Neither can do their work without the other --- and so they have been bred for eons to have that in their make up --- to be anxious to please. Even the worst behaved Labrador cares when mom and dad are annoyed. It is in their DNA to make man happy. Hounds... not so much.

Hounds have been bred for eons to be taken out to the edge of the woods or field and be let loose to go out and do what they do with NO INSTRUCTION from the hunter or handler. They go out and do their thing, all on their own. They make their own decisions and do their own work. And when that work is done and they have found their quarry, they command/call the hunter to come to them with those beautiful voices. (Who is working for whom in that scenario?)

Do you see how your hound thinks differently?

Life with a Hound is far more like having a spouse than a dog. It is far more of a "cooperative effort" with all the give and take that implies. Hounds are not going to do what you say just because you have said it. You are secondary to their desire. There has to be something in it for them. There has to be a trade off. If there is no reward or benefit for the Hound, the Hound cares little what you are asking him/her to do. People incorrectly refer to this as being stubborn - or worse, stupid.

Hounds are actually neither of those things - they are just independent and cunning. They prioritize things differently than do other breeds. They prioritize differently and *you* are not always their priority.

And, this is EXACTLY AS THEY SHOULD BE.

They were bred to be this way. It is all necessary to be a successful hound dog.

When working with a Hound you have to always be thinking:

How do I make myself the priority?

What do I have to give this dog to make me more important than what it smells - or wants?

(and do not expect that anything will ever be 100% successful every time - always be looking for your Hound to act like a Hound.)

We humans always think we are in charge of things. We think that we are top of the chain, the head honcho's...and we naturally approach training our dogs and living with our dogs this way - as though we are in charge.

Your Hound doesn't see it that way.

Your Hound - at best - sees you as a family member or as a sibling (if you are very fortunate - as a parent). Do you walk into your sister or brother's house, start barking orders and they hop to?

Mostly your Hound sees you as a good friend. And what do we do with our friends? When a friend does something for us, we return those favors. There is give and take. When a friendship is out of balance - when one friend takes and takes but does not give - the friendship suffers.

Hounds are happiest when their humans are humble and work with their character. A bond with a hound is not an easy one to create. There is a lot of groundwork involved but when it is established and the balance is there, it's a beautiful thing.

So, if you have a hound or want one, love and appreciate them for what they are and not what they aren't.

(This is a repost from a few different areas on the web where the author is unknown).

"Some of our greatest historical and artistic treasures we place in museums; others, we take for walks."

— Roger Caras

Afghan Hound

Regal, Elegant, Aloof

You could think of an Afghan as a beautiful statue, but they are much more than a majestic accessory. The Afghan is an accomplished athlete and hunter with a keen eye and has such an extraordinary sense of smell that they tend not to accept people that smoke or wear strong perfume. Wary around strangers, they have enormous compassion and care for their people. They need vigorous exercise at least several times a week and adore pastimes such as lure coursing.

History

The Afghan is a truly ancient breed predating written history. Myth says that a pair of Afghans represented dogdom on Noah's Ark. What we do know is that for millennia they were swift and rugged sight-hunting hounds, prized by the kings and princes of Asia's mountain kingdoms.

English officers returning home from the Colonies brought their Afghans with them, where they quickly became beautiful fashion accessories and loyal companions. An early US breeder was Zeppo Marx, the youngest of the Marx Brothers. Pablo Picasso owned an Afghan; he made a giant sculpture of his Kabul which now stands in Daley Plaza, Chicago.

Colors

Colors range widely from black to red to white; black and tan to blue and cream. They can have a black mask, be brindle, brindle domino, or domino. Domino is a specific color pattern that starts with a widow's peak on the head and a clear dark bar running down the top of the muzzle.

By the Numbers

AKC Breed Ranking: 113 out of 197 (2021)

Life expectancy: 12 to 15 years.

Size: 25 to 26 inches, weight: 50 to 60 lbs.

Coat Care: 8 – high; the flowing locks of an Afghan take time and consistency to keep knot-free and beautiful.

Trainability: 3 – low; unless there is chasing involved, an Afghan needs to be convinced that what you want him to do is what he wants to do.

Energy Level: 5 – medium; this breed can loll around in excellent couch potato fashion. But if there is something to chase, the Afghan's energy rises quickly to a 10. The breed does best with regular vigorous exercise.

Good with Children: 5 – medium; they love their people deeply, but can be suspicious of strange children.

Noise Level: 4 – low; they will bark vigorously if necessary; they just don't think that it's often needed.

Shedding Level: 5 – medium; Afghans do shed, but not as much as might be imagined.

Afghan Hound

"No one appreciates the very special genius of your
conversation as the dog does."

— Christopher Morley

American English Coonhound

Intelligent, Tenacious, Loyal

If you happen to look up into a tree one day and spy a big dog with long velvety ears and soulful eyes looking down on you, it's probably an American English Coonhound. They are the only hound that can climb a tree.

The American English is the fastest Coonhound. Mellow at home, friendly with kids, they are tenacious in the woods and live to hunt. They are loud enough to be a great watchdog but have never met a stranger and would kiss a burglar rather than protect hearth and home. As a pack animal, the breed enjoys the company of other dogs.

<u>History</u>

Coonhounds were created to satisfy the American pioneers' need for food and warm coats. The wily raccoon, plentiful in Southern and Midwest woods, provided both meat and fur. And besides, coons were a pest, opening barn doors with sensitive paws and creating havoc within. But racoons were fast and clever and easily evaded the usual hounds. If cornered, they climbed a tree and got away. To create a dog that could hunt down a coon, English hounds brought over by Virginian plantation owners were bred with French hounds brought over by the Marquis de Lafayette and Bloodhounds. Breeders then selected for hardy, tenacious dogs that could chase a coon up a tree and keep the animal cornered until the hunters caught up.

Colors

Red and white ticked, blue and white ticked, tricolor with ticking, red and white, white and black.

By the Numbers

AKC Breed Ranking: 185 out of 197 (2021)

Life expectancy: 11 to 12 years.

Size: 24 to 26 inches (male), 23 to 25 inches (female); weight: 45 to 65 lbs.

Coat Care: 4 – low; American English Coonhounds benefit from an occasional rubdown every once in a while. Vigorous brushing helps when they are shedding.

Trainability: 6 – medium; American English Coonhounds are very easy to train for the things they love to do, like hunting. Other things – not so much. The trick is to convince them that hunting is involved somehow in those things too.

Energy Level: 8 – high; logically, a breed bred to run for hours, chasing down the wily raccoon would need a lot of exercise (if you aren't planning to coonhunt). Hanging around in the backyard won't be enough but chasing a ball for at least 30 minutes can be an excellent source of exercise. The breed does very well as a companion for runners.

Good with Children: 6 – medium; American English Coonhounds enjoy kids, especially when they get to be partners in their adventures.

Noise Level: 8 – high; they have a beautiful and penetrating bay to let the hunter know that they have treed their coon. They use the same bark to let the neighbors know that the moon is full.

Shedding Level: 5 – medium; the breed does shed seasonally.

American English Coonhound

"Dogs laugh, but they laugh with their tails."
— Max Eastman

American Foxhound

Classy, Deep-Mouthed, Persevering, Cheerful

American Foxhounds are good-natured, low maintenance, and great with kids. But the breed's drive to work is so strong that without sufficient outlet, their energy will get taken out on your couch, your dining room table, the front door…….

That beautiful voice will bring tears to the eyes of fox-hunting aficionados. But the neighbors are generally not fox hunting aficionados, and so will have a dim view of a bored American Foxhound's enthusiastic barking.

If the breed has several hours of exercise every day, they can make excellent companions.

History

An avid fox hunter, George Washington imported sturdy Foxhounds from England for his pack. But the dogs couldn't perform well; the wilder American terrain needed an agile and swift animal. Washington improved his pack with French dogs given him by his friend, the Marquis of Lafayette and the germ of today's American Foxhound was born.

<u>**Colors**</u>

American Foxhounds can be any color, per their Standard, but are generally a tricolor of black, white, and tan.

<u>**By the Numbers**</u>

AKC Breed Ranking: 186 out of 197 (2021)

Life expectancy: 12 to 15 years.

Size: 22 to 26 inches (male), 21 to 24 inches (female); weight: 65 to 70 lbs. (male), 60 to 65 lbs. (female)

Coat Care: 4 – low; American Foxhounds benefit from a good brushing if they are shedding and need a bath only when they have managed to get themselves covered with mud.

Trainability: 5 – medium; they are amicable and willing but not always biddable. They do best in sports that showcase their native abilities.

Energy Level: 9 – high; logically, a breed bred to run for hours, following the scent of a fox through wood and field is going to be extremely high energy. The breed does surprisingly well as a companion for runners.

Good with Children: 8 – high; American Foxhounds love kids, and kids love them.

Noise Level: 9 – high; the breed has a beautiful "bay", bred to let the huntsman know the fox is near. Of course, that loud beautiful bark also informs in detail about the squirrels in the back yard, the full moon, and the neighbor walking by.

Shedding Level: 7 – medium; American Foxhounds shed a surprisingly high amount seasonally.

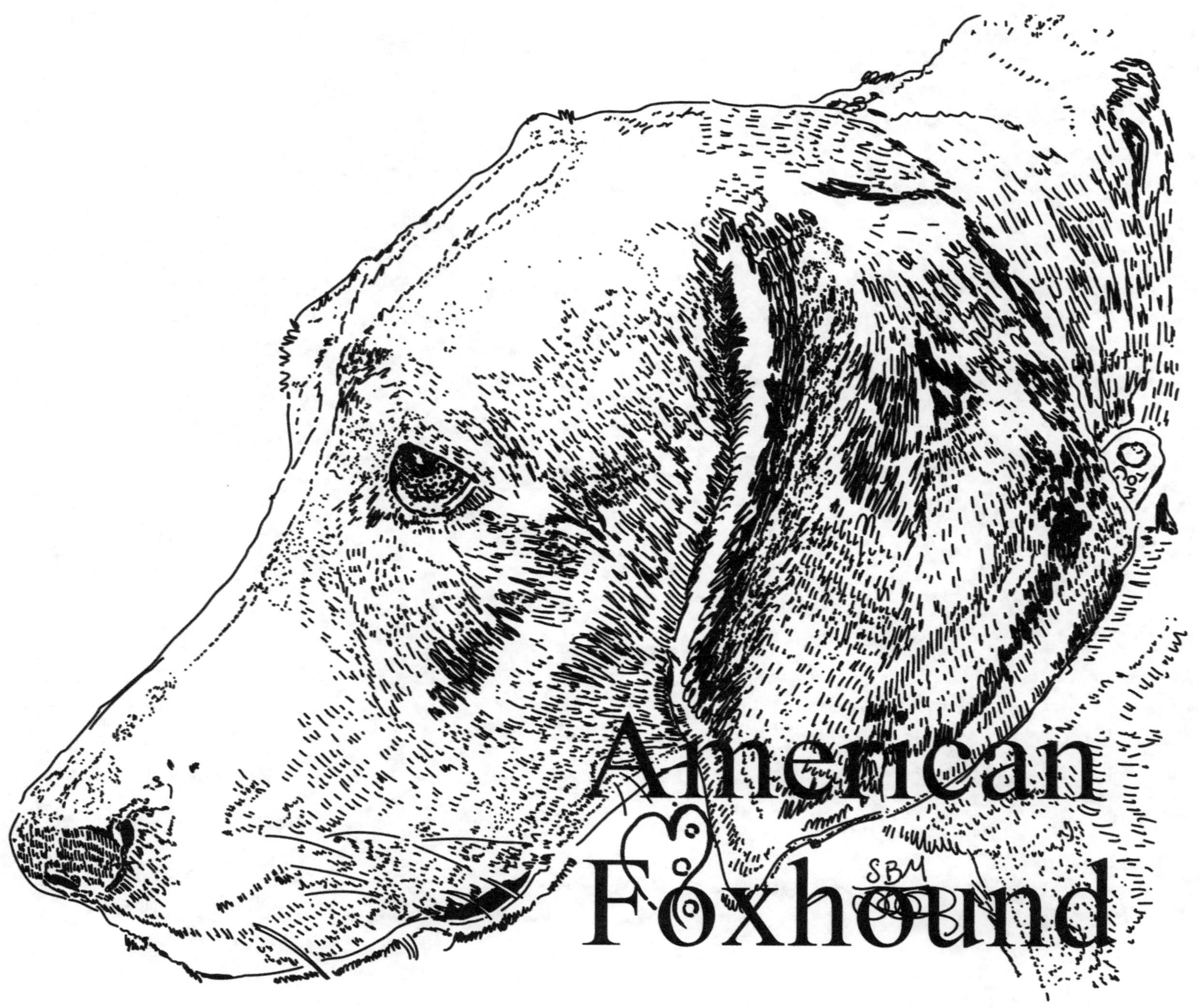

American
Foxhound

"The greatest pleasure of a dog is that you may make a fool of yourself with him and not only will he not scold you, but he will make a fool of himself too."

— Samuel Butler

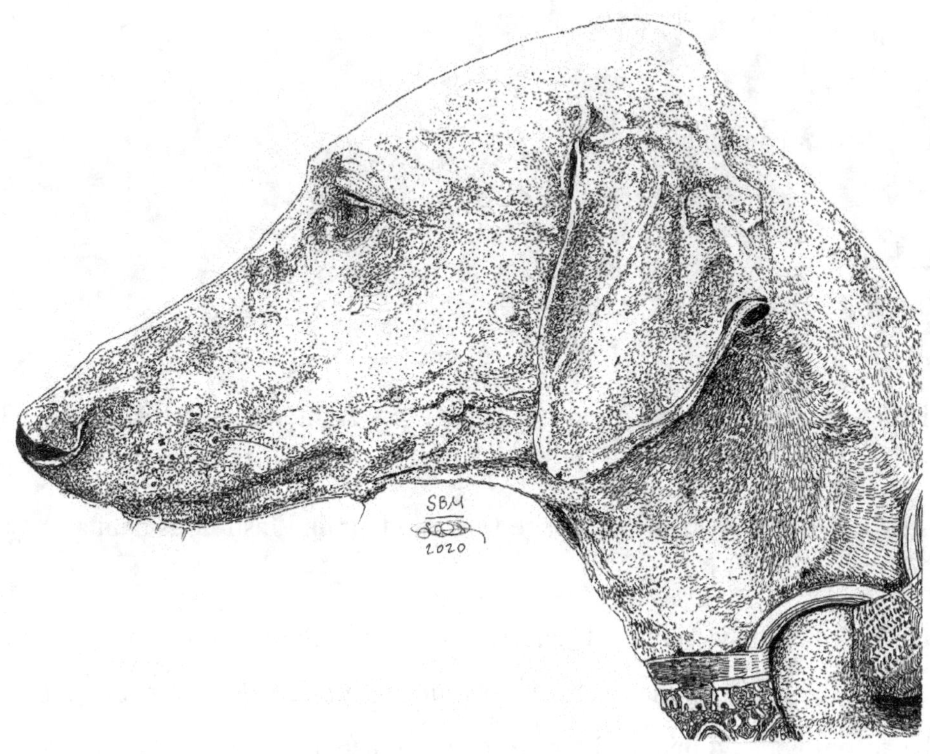

Azawakh

Devoted, Vigilant, Discerning

The Azawakh is a West African sighthound, used to hunt antelope in the broken terrain of the southern Sahara. Elegant and exotically beautiful, he is healthiest when thin enough to see his hipbones. More moderate than some of the other sighthounds, he floats when he gaits. If you want a dog that resembles a gazelle, an Azawakh might be right for you.

Like all sighthounds, the Azawakh needs plenty of exercise, at least 30 minutes of walkies every day without fail. As desert dogs, their coat is thin and fine, and they have trouble tolerating cold climates. Azawakhs adore their people but can be suspicious of strangers. They are fine with older children but are too sensitive to tolerate the shenanigans of young kids.

History

The Azawakh comes from arid West Africa and has long been a devoted and valued companion to the

Tuareg people, a nomadic group living in the South Sahara. They have been deeply devoted to their people and valuable as avid hunters for thousands of years.

Colors

Can be any color or color combination.

By the Numbers

AKC Breed Ranking: 193 out of 197 (2021)

Life expectancy: 12 to 15 years.

Size: 25 to 29 inches (male), 23.5 to 27.5 inches (female); weight: 44 to 55 lbs. (male) 33 to 44 lbs. (female).

Coat Care: 2 – extremely low; Azawakh's have fine thin hair and fastidious habits; they stay clean even after a hard day in the field.

Trainability: 6 – medium; they enjoy and learn well activities like lure coursing, which they excel at.

Energy Level: 8 – high; this is an ancient breed intended to hunt all day over rough terrain. That energy level needs to be accommodated in a pet home or they can become depressed or destructive.

Good with Children: 5 – medium; they love their own older children deeply but are sensitive and don't like being mauled by kids too young to know better.

Noise Level: 4 – low; they will bark vigorously if necessary; they just don't think that it's often needed.

Shedding Level: 4 – medium; though Azawakhs do shed, their coat is light and fine.

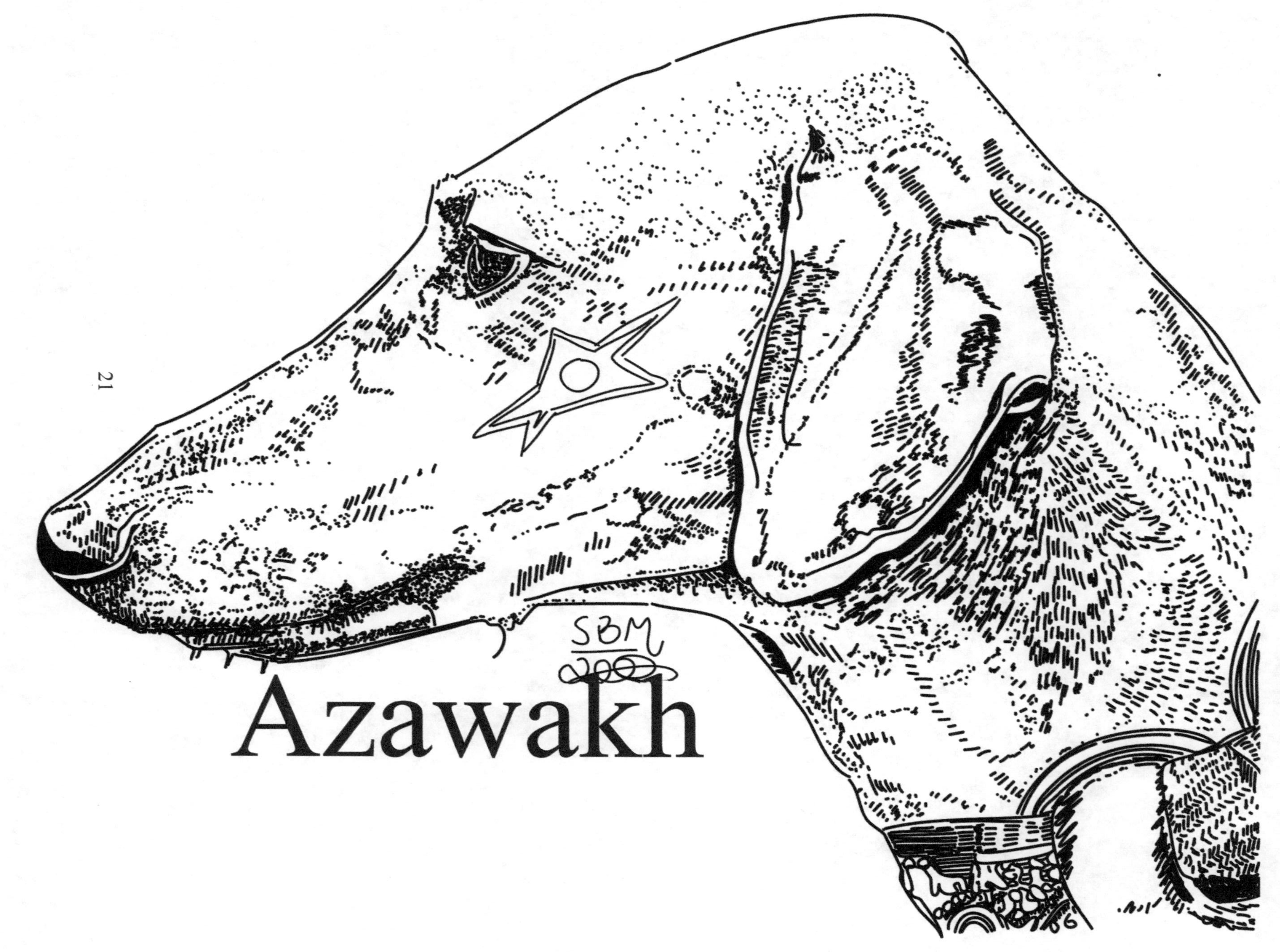

Azawakh

"These dogs, notwithstanding their wildness, do little or no damage to the inhabitants. They are red-haired, have small slender bodies and their tails turned upon their backs."

— Father Jerome Merolla, 17th-century Catholic missionary to the Congo

Basenji

Agile, Alert, Springy

The Basenji is a breed untouched by history. Living semi-wild for thousands of years in the Congo, they clean themselves like a cat and yodel rather than bark. The African name for the breed translates to "the-jumping-up-and-down-dog".

Basenjis do things on their agenda. They are aloof with strangers and don't care to be approached from behind. But they love their people and are surprisingly tolerant of children. As hunters used to long hours work outside, they need plenty of exercise.

The face wrinkles make a Basenji look permanently slightly worried, but don't let that fool you. They are calm and self-assured.

History

Like many of their hound counterparts, the Basenji is an ancient breed. Paleontologists say that the first domesticated dogs look a lot like Basenjis. The breed was depicted in Egyptian hieroglyphs and can also be seen in Babylonian and Mesopotamian artifacts.

Those civilizations didn't last but the Basenji did, escaping to the headwaters of the Congo and Nile and going semi-wild. They were versatile hunters, operating by both sight and scent. They could muster explosive bursts of speed and had an extraordinary ability to leap vertically into the air.

Dogs were brought out of the Congo in the late 1800's and after several false starts, was established in the US and England. Additional dogs were brought from the Congo 25 years ago, expanding the gene pool and improving the health of the breed.

Colors

Chestnut, black, tricolor, or brindle.

By the Numbers

AKC Breed Ranking: 86 out of 197 (2021)

Life expectancy: 13 to 14 years.

Size: 17 inches (male), 16 inches (female); weight: 24 lbs. (male), 22 lbs. (female)

Coat Care: 4 – low; Basenjis benefit from a good brushing if they are shedding and need a bath only when they have managed to get themselves covered with mud. Like a cat, they enjoy licking themselves clean.

Trainability: 6 – medium; they are smart dogs adaptable to many situations. They do need to feel that what you want them to do was their idea all along.

Energy Level: 8 – high; logically, a breed bred to run for hours hunting by sight and scent, will be high energy. The breed does surprisingly well as a companion for runners. They don't do well around small family pets like gerbils or guinea pigs.

Good with Children: 7 – medium; Basenjis love kids, and kids love them.

Noise Level: 2 – low; the breed has a chortle or yodel to verbalize, but that doesn't carry like barking.

Shedding Level: 5 – medium; Basenjis do shed seasonally.

Basenji

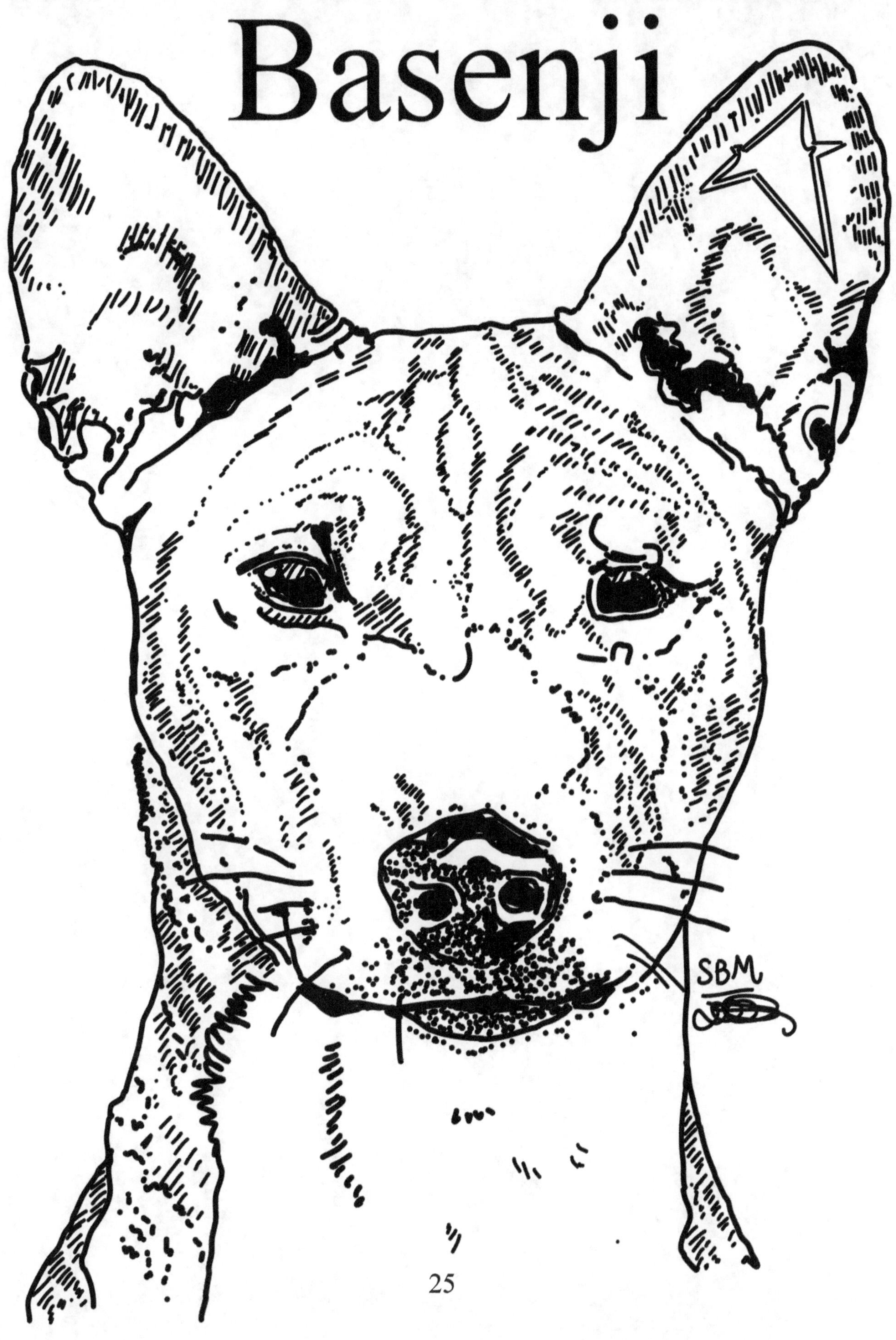

"Properly trained, a man can be a dog's best friend."

— Corey Ford

Basset Hound

Stubborn, Affectionate, Great Sense of Smell

The Basset Hound is the quiet gentleman of dogdom. A big dog with short legs, the Basset is tireless on the hunt and his nose is only second to the Bloodhound. But when not working, the Basset is most excellent at relaxing. He is gentle and tolerant of children but may be too quiet to be an active kid's companion. If you are looking for a relaxed buddy that epitomizes the definition of "chill", a Basset Hound may be right for you.

Like all drop-eared breeds, care must be taken to keep the long velvety ears clean, as the warm damp climate invites fungus and bacteria.

History

Friars at the Abbey of St. Hubert, close to Namur in today's southern Belgium, wanted to create a low-slung dog (Basset is French for low) who was a tireless hunter but slow enough to be followed by a hunter on foot. Their accuracy and persistence made them a popular hunting hound with French aristocrats.

There's some evidence that the Marquis of Lafayette gave George Washington Basset Hounds.

Colors

All hound colors are acceptable, ranging from black and white to lemon and white to tricolor.

By the Numbers

AKC Breed Ranking: 36 out of 197 (2021)

Life expectancy: 12 to 13 years.

Size: up to 15 inches; 40 to 65 lbs.

Coat Care: 4 – low; Basset Hounds benefit from a good brushing if they are shedding and need a bath only when they have managed to get themselves covered with mud.

Trainability: 5 – medium; they are eager to learn more about what they do well; tracking something by scent. They have good house manners but it's tough to get them excited about the various performance events.

Energy Level: 3 – low; the Basset is famously relaxed when not hunting. When tracking a scent he is slow but tireless.

Good with Children: 6 – medium; Basset Hounds like kids but run out of energy quickly.

Noise Level: 6 – medium; Bassets don't bark a lot, as they don't consider it their job to be a watchdog. But when they do let loose it's loud and ringing.

Shedding Level: 5 – medium; Basset Hounds do shed seasonally.

Basset

Hound

27

"A dog desires affection more than it's dinner. Well -- almost." — Charlotte Gray

Beagle

Big for Inches, Perfect Family Pet,

Foxhound in Miniature

Beagles are the ultimate kid dog. Let a Beagle loose in a house full of people and he will find the children and hang out with them. As a pack hound, he is friendly with other dogs and enjoys canine company. Friendly and cheerful, he also remains a scenthound and will follow the smell of a rabbit across three counties.
He is not hypoallergenic and special care needs to be taken of his velvety ears to keep them free of infection.

History

Long before the Romans headed for England, there are reports of small pack-hounds. In the 1500's he was called the "foothound of our country, indigenous to the soil."
Unlike the larger pack hounds, Beagles could be hunted on foot. This was perfect for people who could afford to keep a couple of dogs but couldn't afford to keep horses.
Beagles arrived in the US after the Civil War and were quickly embraced by rabbit hunters. "Beaglers"

even today swear by the breed's nose. Beagles are the most popular Hound breed which is easy to understand with their friendliness and great hunting ability.

Colors

All hound colors are acceptable, ranging from black and white to lemon and white to tricolor.

By the Numbers

AKC Breed Ranking: 7 out of 197 (2021)

Life expectancy: 10 to 15 years.

Size: under 20 lbs. (13 inches and under); 20 to 30 lbs. (13 to 15 inches).

Coat Care: 4 – low; Beagles benefit from a good brushing a couple of times a week to keep the shedding under control. They need a bath if they manage to get themselves covered with mud.

Trainability: 6 – medium; Beagles are extremely food motivated. It's like they have a sign around their neck: "Will work for kibble". But they are easily distracted, and if outside, any squirrel crossing their path will win over any amount of training. They never should be let off-leash in open areas.

Energy Level: 7 – medium; they require plenty of exercise but adore playing with their people and other dogs.

Good with Children: 10 – very high; this breed is the penultimate kid dog.

Noise Level: 7 – medium; Beagles don't bark a lot, as they don't consider it their job to be a watchdog. But when they do let loose it's a loud and ringing bay.

Shedding Level: 7 – medium; Beagles have a thick double coat that builds up over the winter and drops in the spring. They also shed all year round.

Beagle

"When an 85 lb. mammal licks your tears away, then tries to sit in your lap, it's hard to feel sad." — Kristan Higgins

Black and Tan Coonhound

Laid Back, Deep "Bawl", Most Excellent Nose

The Black and Tan Coonhound is a big friendly goofball; he is easygoing and loves the company of other dogs and people. But when there is work to be done, the Black and Tan is all business – he is a tenacious hunter who can follow an old scent almost as well as a fresh one.

He is not hypoallergenic and special care needs to be taken of his velvety ears to keep them free of infection.

History

Coonhounds were created to satisfy the American pioneers' need for food and warm coats. The wily raccoon, plentiful in Southern and Midwest woods, provided both meat and fur. And besides, coons were a pest, opening barn doors with sensitive paws and creating havoc within. But racoons were fast and clever and easily evaded the usual hounds. If cornered, they climbed a tree and got away. To create a dog that could hunt down a coon, English hounds brought over by Virginian plantation owners were bred with French hounds brought over by the Marquis de Lafayette and Bloodhounds. Breeders then selected for hardy, tenacious dogs that could chase a coon up a tree and keep the animal cornered until the hunters caught up.

Daniel Boone and Davy Crockett were both Black and Tan Coonhound enthusiasts. Daniel Boone said: "My favorite of all hounds are those of dark colors, primarily of black and tan."

Colors

Coal-black with rich tan markings above eyes, on sides of muzzle, chest, legs, and breeching, with black pencil markings on toes.

By the Numbers

AKC Breed Ranking: 127 out of 197 (2021).

Life expectancy: 10 to 12 years.

Size: 25 to 27 inches (male); 23 to 25 inches (female); weight: 65 to 110 lbs.

Coat Care: 4 – low; Black and Tan Coonhounds benefit from a good brushing to keep the shedding under control. They need a bath if they manage to get themselves covered with mud, and special and regular attention needs to be paid to their ears.

Trainability: 5 – medium; Black and Tans are independent and can be insistent on doing things their way. They never should be let off-leash in open areas. They easily learn anything that has to do with hunting or tracking.

Energy Level: 7 – medium; they require plenty of exercise but adore playing with their people and other dogs.

Good with Children: 8 – high; they enjoy children and can tolerate kid shenanigans.

Noise Level: 7 – medium; Black and Tan Coonhounds don't bark a lot, as they don't consider it their job to be a watchdog. But when they do let loose it's a loud and ringing bay. If lonely they will let the neighborhood know how they feel.

Shedding Level: 7 – medium; Black and Tan Coonhounds shed seasonally.

37

Black and Tan Coonhound

"You can usually tell that a man is good if he has a
dog who loves him."
— W. Bruce Cameron

Bloodhound

The Nose Knows, A Voice Like No Other

When a child goes missing, when a criminal escapes, rescue workers and police don't use apps or fancy equipment; they call in "the dogs". And by dogs, they mean….Bloodhounds. No fancy equipment has ever been made that surpasses the nose and the tenacity of a Bloodhound. When you talk about this breed you have to start with his nose, which consists of approximately 230 million olfactory cells: 40 times the number in humans.

When not working this is a relaxed breed, mellow and laid back. If you ask a Bloodhound, "Want to play?" a Bloodhound's answer will be "Maybe later." Unless there is exploring to do; then he's "Let's go!"
He is not hypoallergenic and special care needs to be taken of his velvety ears to keep them free of infection. The breed is also a drool machine and leaves a patch of damp wherever he lies.
History

The background of the Bloodhound began with the patron saint of hunting, a French monk named Hubert in the 7th century. He combined strains from various great houses – that's why the breed is called "blooded" meaning coming from aristocratic lineage. In the 16th century Bloodhounds became known for man trailing and trails performed by proven Bloodhounds are permissible in court.

Colors

Black and tan, liver and tan, and red.

By the Numbers

AKC Breed Ranking: 46 out of 197 (2021)

Life expectancy: 10 to 12 years.

Size: 25 to 27 inches (male); 23 to 25 inches (female); weight: 90 to 110 lbs. (male), 80 to 100 lbs. (female).

Coat Care: 4 – low; Bloodhounds benefit from a good brushing to keep the shedding under control. They need a bath if they manage to get themselves covered with mud, and special and regular attention needs to be paid to their ears. It's smart to have small towels nearby to control the drool.

Trainability: 7 – medium; Bloodhounds can be independent and should never should be let off-leash in open areas. They easily learn anything that has to do with tracking. This is a breed that lives for his nose; he needs to use that skill.

Energy Level: 6 – medium; they need plenty of exercise but have a definite off switch; they are also champion couch potatoes.

Good with Children: 6 – medium; they enjoy children but are so laid back they'd rather snooze on the couch than play with the kids. They do love to go exploring but need a child strong enough to control them. This is a big dog that sometimes demands to dive into the bushes, following a scent.

Noise Level: 8 – high; When Bloodhounds they do let loose it's a loud and ringing bay. If lonely or bored they will let the neighborhood know how they feel.

Shedding Level: 7 – medium; Bloodhounds shed seasonally.

Bloodhound

"The most affectionate creature in the world is a wet dog." — Ambrose Bierce

Bluetick Coonhound

Musical Voice, Resolute, Steady

The Bluetick Coonhound is a friendly energetic dog always up for the next adventure. He has one of the strongest prey drives of all the coonhounds; he is a tenacious hunter who can follow an old scent almost as well as a fresh one. In a home that allows the Bluetick to expend his energy, either with hunting or being an active companion including several hours of walking or running every day, he can be a laid back and friendly buddy.

He is not hypoallergenic and special care needs to be taken of his velvety ears to keep them free of infection.

History

Coonhounds were created to satisfy the American pioneers' need for food and warm coats. The wily raccoon, plentiful in Southern and Midwest woods, provided both meat and fur. And besides, coons were a pest, opening barn doors with sensitive paws and creating havoc within. But racoons were fast and clever and easily evaded the usual hounds. If cornered, they climbed a tree and got away. To create a dog that could hunt down a coon, English hounds brought over by Virginian plantation owners were bred with French hounds brought over by the Marquis de Lafayette and Bloodhounds. Breeders then selected for hardy, tenacious dogs that could chase a coon up a tree and keep the animal cornered until the hunters caught up.

Colors

Either blue ticked or blue ticked and tan, predominantly black on the head.

By the Numbers

AKC Breed Ranking: 137 out of 197 (2021)

Life expectancy: 11 to 12 years.

Size: 22 to 27 inches (male); 21 to 25 inches (female); weight: 55 to 80 lbs. (male), 45 to 65 lbs. (female).

Coat Care: 4 – low; Bluetick Coonhounds benefit from a good brushing to keep the shedding under control. They need a bath if they manage to get themselves covered with mud, and special and regular attention needs to be paid to their ears.

Trainability: 7 – medium; Bluetick are more eager to please than other Coonhounds – they want to do right by their people. They are open to training in non-tracking pursuits. But they are still devoted hunters and should never be let off-leash in open areas.

Energy Level: 8 – high; they require plenty of exercise but adore playing with their people and other dogs.

Good with Children: 8 – high; they enjoy children and can tolerate kid shenanigans.

Noise Level: 7 – medium; Bluetick Coonhounds don't bark a lot, as they don't consider it their job to be a watchdog. But when they do let loose it's a loud and ringing bay. If lonely or bored they will serenade the neighborhood.

Shedding Level: 7 – medium; Bluetick Coonhounds shed seasonally.

Bluetick
Coonhound

"It's just the most amazing thing to love a dog, isn't it?
It makes our relationships with people seem as boring
as oatmeal." — John Grogan

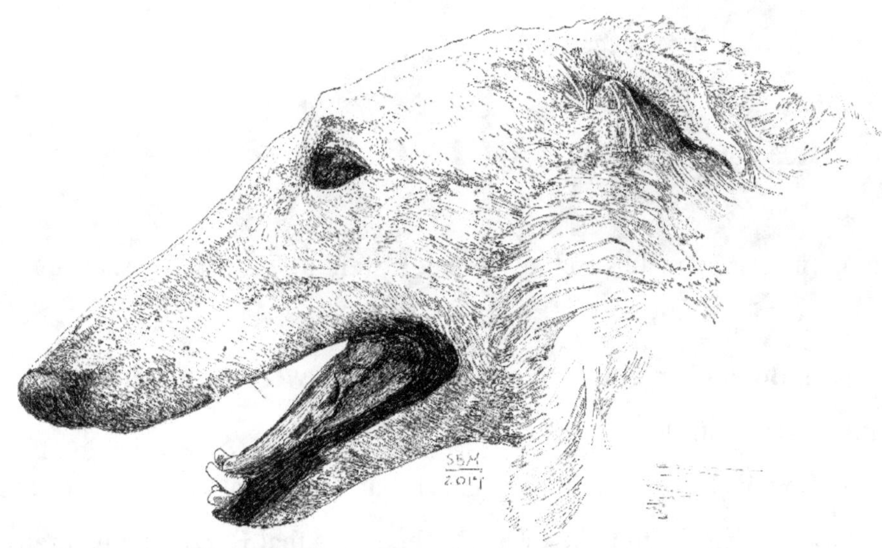

Borzoi

Elegant, Aloof with Strangers, Graceful Hunter

Borzoi are one of those breeds which effortlessly command their surroundings. Regal and quiet, they draw attention and fill the eye. Self-confident without being pushy, a Borzoi knows what he wants and calmly sets out to get it. This can make training a challenge, and he is one of those breeds that need to feel that what you want him to do is what he wanted to do all along.

As a sight hunter, he does not mesh well with small mammals like gerbils or rabbits, as their quick movements can waken the Borzoi's hunting instincts. The breed enjoys children but prefers to watch their antics from the sidelines.

As with all giant breeds, strenuous exercise should be avoided after eating, as they can bloat (where the stomach twists, needing immediate emergency surgery).

History

The Borzoi was created for the Russian nobles in the late 1600s by breeding Greyhounds and a thick-coated, now extinct giant breed. Swift like a Greyhound, Borzoi worked in packs of 100 dogs or more, primarily hunting wolves.

This gentle giant of a breed was slaughtered wholesale during the Russian Revolution as they were a symbol of the hated aristocracy. However, enough dogs had been imported to England (where Queen Alexandra was an avid supporter) and the US to ensure their survival.

<u>**Colors**</u>

Any color or combination of colors is acceptable.

<u>**By the Numbers**</u>

AKC Breed Ranking: 103 out of 197 (2021)

Life expectancy: 9 to 14 years.

Size: 28 inches and up (male); 26 inches and up (female); weight: 75 to 105 lbs. (male), 60 to 85 lbs. (female).

Coat Care: 5 – medium; Borzoi benefits from a good brushing every week to tame tangles and to keep the seasonal shedding under control.

Trainability: 4 – low; Borzois know what they want. If that's not what you want, it can be a challenge to bring them around to your way of thinking. The good news is that Borzoi are naturally sweet-tempered, quiet, and clean, so going along with what they want is not usually that hard.

Energy Level: 5 – medium; they are generally elegant couch potatoes unless they see something to hunt. Then they are a 10 in energy, and should never be let off-leash in an open area.

Good with Children: 6 – medium; they enjoy children but prefer to watch their shenanigans from the sidelines.

Noise Level: 2 – low; Borzoi rarely bark.

Shedding Level: 7 – medium; Borzoi shed seasonally.

Borzoi

"Dogs have a way of finding the people who need them, filling an emptiness we don't even know we have." — Thom Jones

Cirneco dell'Etna

Elegant, Athletic, Suave

The Cirneco dell'Etna ("cheer-NEK-o") is one of those breeds you can't stop staring at. It's the coat –
an eye-catching warm chestnut. They are the smallest primitive sighthound and hail from Sicily.
Because they are hard-wired to be fabulous sprinters, Cirnechi need plenty of exercise including a daily
chance to stretch out and run. It's no surprise they love lure coursing, but failing that, the chance to
chase down a ball every day is critical.

As a sight hunter the Cirneco dell'Etna does not mesh well with small mammals like gerbils or rabbits;
their quick movements can waken the Cirneco dell'Etna's hunting instincts. The breed enjoys children
in moderation – they don't tolerate kid shenanigans well.

As housedogs Cirnechi make gentle and loyal companions.

History

The name Cirneco comes from a Greek word meaning "dog of Cyrene (Libya)".

It looks like the breed has existed in Sicily for over 3000 years, brought to its shores by the master tradesmen of the Mediterranean, the Phoenicians. There are Sicilian coins from 500 BC with the small dog on them. The breed has been there ever since, chasing hare and game birds across the rocky slopes of Mount Etna.

By the 1930s the Cirneco was almost extinct. Dr. Maurizio Migneco DVM wrote an article about them, which was seen by Baroness Agata Paterno Castello, a Sicilian aristocrat. She decided to take on the revival of the breed and made this her life's work. The breed was recognized by Italy's national kennel club in 1939, and by the AKC in 2015.

Colors

Chestnut.

By the Numbers

AKC Breed Ranking: 179 out of 197 (2021)

Life expectancy: 12 to 14 years.

Size: 18 to 19.5 inches (male); 16.5 to 18 inches (female); weight: 22 to 26 lbs. (male), 17 to 22lbs. (female).

Coat Care: 2 – low; Cirnechi enjoy a rub down, especially when shedding, but rarely need a bath.

Trainability: 7 – medium; Cirnechi know what they want but are willing to compromise. They are one of the most biddable sighthounds, probably because they enjoy spending time with their people.

Energy Level: 7 – medium; this is a breed that can work hard in harsh conditions. That's high energy. But they also know how to relax. Given enough walks or a good run every day, or plenty of ball chasing – they also love sports like lure coursing -- they are mellow and accommodating family members.

Good with Children: 6 – medium; they enjoy calm children and make good buddies for adventures.

Noise Level: 2 – low; Cirnechi rarely bark.

Shedding Level: 5 – medium; Cirnechi shed seasonally.

Cirneco dell'Etna

"Once you have had a wonderful dog, a life without
one is a life diminished."

— Dean Koontz

Dachshund

Feisty, Fearless, Funny

Long, Low and Lovable

My introduction to this breed was less than perfect. As a teenager I was at a friend's house for a party. In wandered the resident Wirehaired Dachshund, self-assured and entitled. He spied my long and somewhat smelly shoelaces and decided they were a delicacy. When I tried to move away, he growled. And meant it. That dog kept me in lockdown for at least 20 minutes as he extracted every bit of goodness he could from my shoelaces. When he was done, he wandered off happy and ignored me the rest of the evening. I learned my first Dachshund lesson: Dachsies know what they want and aren't afraid to demand it!

<u>History</u>

600 years ago, tunnel burrowing badgers (called "Dachs" in German) ranged over what is now southern Germany. A dog was needed to control their spread. He needed to be long and low to fit underground with ease and have formidable digging abilities. He also needed to be fearless; up to the task of taking on the badger's size, long claws, and sharp teeth. And so the Dachshund was born.

<u>Colors and Coats</u>

Dachshunds come in 6 varieties; smooth, wirehaired, and longhaired; each comes in standard and miniature. They are so popular in Europe that every variety is considered a breed in themselves and are part of their own Group at dog shows. They have a wide range of possible colors, from red through black and tan, with markings equally wide range from dapple through sable to brindle.

By the Numbers

AKC Breed Ranking: 12 out of 197 (2021)

Life Expectancy: 12 – 16 years

Size: 8 – 9 inches (Standard), 5 – 6 inches (Miniature); weight: 16 – 32 lbs. (Standard), 11 lbs and under (Miniature)

Coat Care: Wirehaired: 7 – medium; they need regular hand stripping (where the dead undercoat is pulled out by hand) or clippering to stay tidy.

> **Smooth Coat: 2 – low**

> **Longhaired: 5 – medium;** they need regular brushing to loosen dead hair and take care of tangles.

All three varieties benefit from regular baths – Dachshunds are adventurous and enjoy getting into anything dirty or smelly. Also, special and regular care must be taken of their long ears to keep them sweet-smelling and free of infection.

Trainability: 6 – medium; Dachshunds can be trained, especially if they think something is their idea in the first place. They are a 10 in trainability in all Earthdog and Barn Hunt events and adore going underground.

Energy Level: 7 – medium; Dachshunds can be mellow couch potatoes. But if hunting, they can be tireless.

Good With Children: 6 – medium; they do very well with older children who understand what a Dachshund wants he should get.

Noise Level: 8 – high; this is a noisy breed, bred to bark loud enough to be heard when hunting underground.

Shedding Level: Wirehaired: 3 – low; they are non-shedding

> **Smooth Coat: 5 – medium**

> **Longhaired: 7 – medium;** but the hair they shed is longer

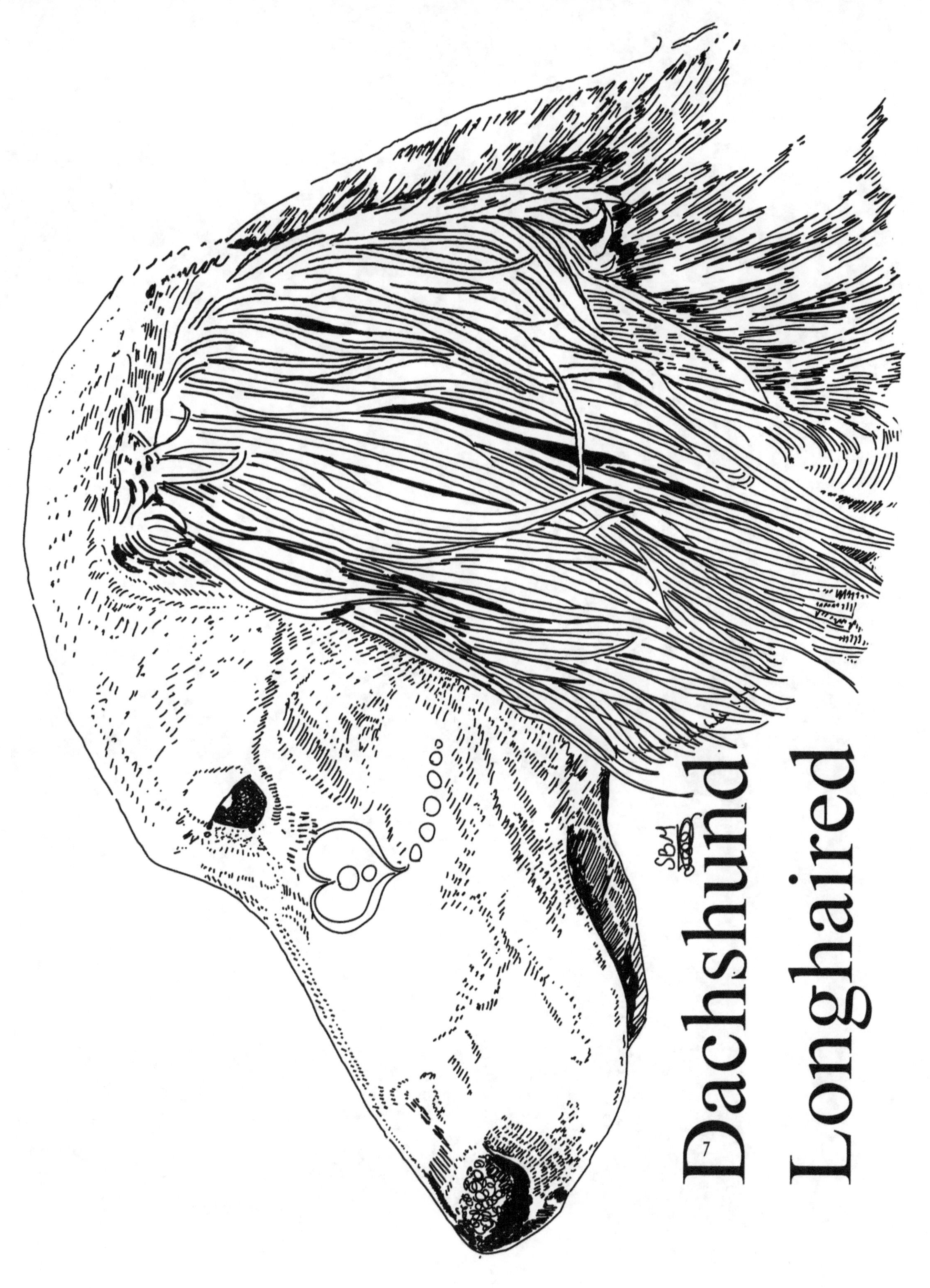

Dachshund
Longhaired

Dachshund Smooth

Dachshund Wirehaired

"There is no faith which has never been broken,
except that of a truly faithful dog."

— Konrad Lorenz

English Foxhound

Friendly Working Hound

English Foxhounds are good natured, low maintenance and great with kids. But the breed's drive to work is so strong that without sufficient outlet, their energy will get taken out on your couch, your dining room table, the front door…….

That beautiful voice will bring tears to the eyes of fox hunting aficionados. But the neighbors are generally not fox hunting aficionados, and so will have a dim view of a bored English Foxhound's enthusiastic barking.

If not actively hunting, the English Foxhound can excel as a runner's companion. But this is not a breed for an inexperienced owner. As a pack animal, he enjoys the company of other dogs.

History

As the dark ages waned, England's countryside slowly morphed from dense woods to rolling hills and farms. Aristocracy's need for hunting dogs morphed as well, from sturdy giant animals able to chase and take down the big British stag, to dogs capable of zigging and zagging over field and fence after the wily farmer's pest – the fox.

George Washington was an avid foxhunter, and along with fellow plantation owners imported

English foxhounds to fuel his passion in the US. English foxhounds are behind American Foxhounds and the various Coonhounds.

Colors

English Foxhounds can be any color, as long as it's a combination of a good "hound" color, that is black, tan or white.

By the Numbers

AKC Breed Ranking: 188 out of 197 (2021)

Life expectancy: 10 to 13 years.

Size: 24 inches; weight: 60 to 75 lbs.

Coat Care: 4 – low; English Foxhounds benefit from a good rub down occasionally.

Trainability: 4 – low; they are amiable and willing but not vey biddable. They do best in sports that showcase their native abilities.

Energy Level: 9 – high; it's pretty logical that a breed bred to gallop for hours, following the scent of a fox through field and stream is going to be extremely high energy. The English Foxhound does surprisingly well as a companion for runners.

Good with Children: 8 – high; English Foxhounds love kids, and kids love them.

Noise Level: 9 – high; the breed has a beautiful "bay", bred to let the huntsman know the fox is near. Of course, that loud beautiful bark can also inform in detail about the squirrels in the back yard, the full moon and the neighbors walking by.

Shedding Level: 7 – medium; English Foxhounds shed seasonally.

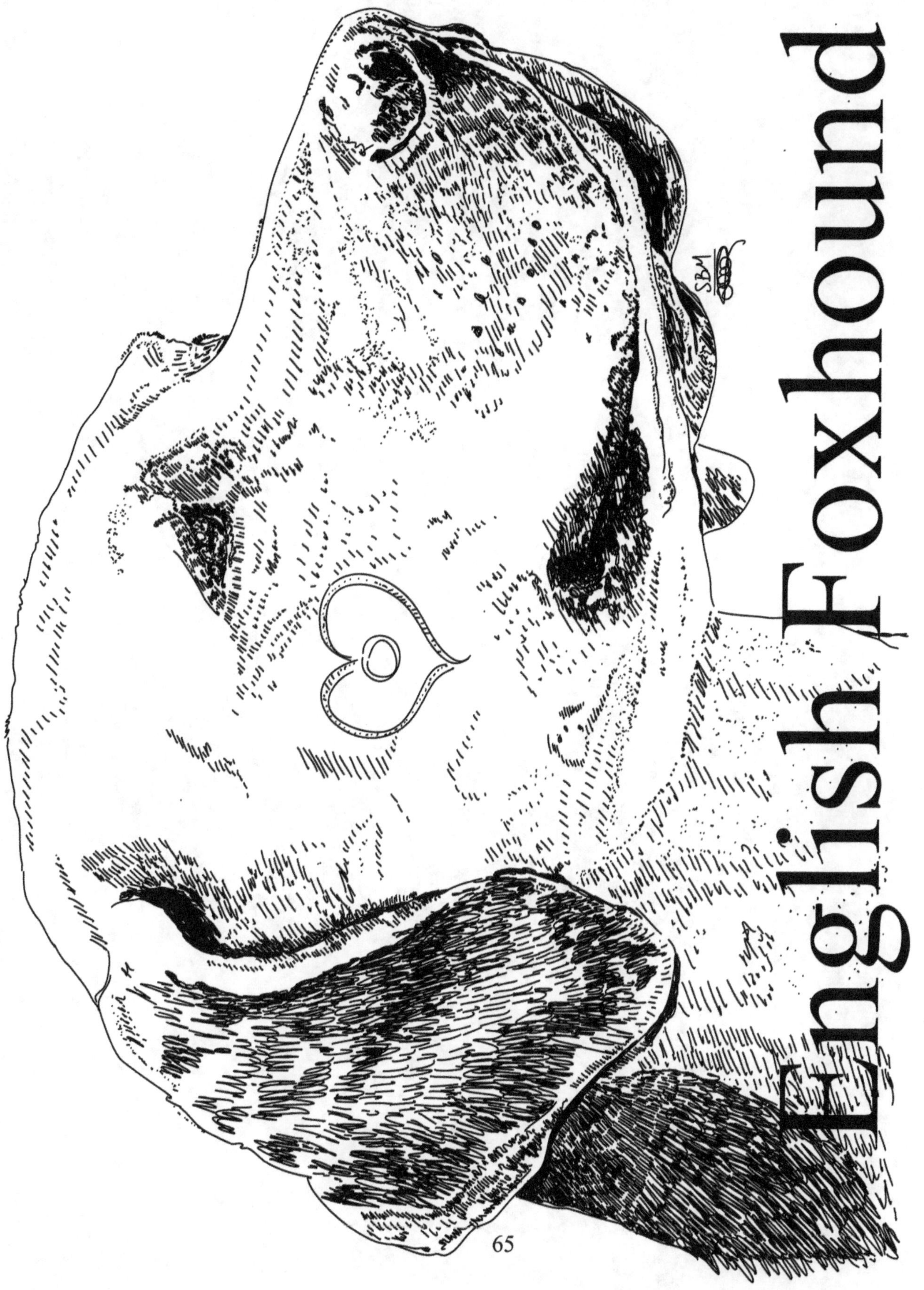

English Foxhound

"If you think dogs can't count, try putting three dog biscuits in your pocket and then only give him two of them." — Phil Pastoret

Grand Bassett Griffon Vendeen

Scruffy Eared Clown, Independent, Cheerful, Social

The Grand Basset Griffon Vendeen is a medium-sized scruffy clown who loves to play – until there is something to trail. Then he is all business. His rough wiry coat protects him from the briars and thorns of his native countryside – the coastal Vendeen, south of Brittany.

Care must be taken of his long velvety ears to keep them clean and healthy, and he does shed.

The breed gets along well with kids and enjoys the company of other dogs.

<u>History</u>

The creation of the Griffon Vendeen family started at least 400 years ago when French King Louis' Master of Hounds (called the "Greffier") crossed the Griffon de Bresse (a wheat-coated, rough-coated hound) with the royal white smooth coated hunting dogs. The two smallest Griffon breeds thus created were the Petit Basset (25 to 40 lbs.) and the Grand Basset. They were Basset (low to the ground) and moved slower, so people could follow them on foot.

The Petit Basset Griffon Vendeen was bred to hunt rabbit, the Grand Basset Griffon Vendeen to hunt hare and boar.

Colors

GBGVs are mostly white with any other color, or black and tan.

By the Numbers

AKC Breed Ranking: 188 out of 197 (2021)

Life expectancy: 13 to 15 years.

Size: 15.5 to 18 inches; weight: 40 to 45 lbs.

Coat Care: 5 – medium; regular brushing helps keep the burrs out and the tangles tamed.

Trainability: 6 – medium; Grand Basset Griffon Vendeens enjoy learning if it has to do with hunting or trailing by scent.

Energy Level: 8 – high; they're a playful breed and enjoy nothing more than romping with their people.

Good with Children: 8 – high; they enjoy children of all ages and are down with any mischief the kids might dream up.

Noise Level: 7 – medium; the breed is a good watchdog and will let you know what's going on. Sometimes you'll want to hear all about the latest, sometimes not so much. They make a poor guard dog as they love everyone, even the burglar come to steal the silver.

Shedding Level: 6 – medium; Grand Basset Griffon Vendeens do shed.

Grand Basset Griffon Vendeen

"You can tell by the kindness of a dog how a human should be." — Captain Beefheart

Greyhound

Would Rather Be Chasing Something

The Greyhound is the fastest dog alive – they can sprint up to 45 mph. Compare that to the fastest human (Usain Bolt) whose record is 27.8 mph. You would think that such a fast animal would be hyper and nervous, but nothing is further from the truth. Greyhounds are laid back loungers, happy to match the carpet all day long – unless there is something to chase. Then they come alive.

Because they are hard wired to be fabulous sprinters, the breed does need plenty of exercise including the chance to really stretch out and run. It's no surprise they love lure coursing, but failing that, the chance to chase down a ball every day is critical.

As a sight hunter the Greyhound does not mesh well with small mammals like gerbils or rabbits; their quick movements can waken the Greyhound's hunting instincts. The breed enjoys children but prefers to watch their antics from the sidelines.

As with all giant breeds, strenuous exercise should be avoided after eating, as they can bloat (where the stomach twists, needing immediate emergency surgery).

<u>**History**</u>

The Greyhound is an ancient breed; 5000 years ago, the Egyptian pharaohs coursed them in the Sahara. Ever after, rulers have known that they looked a bit more noble with a swift and elegant Greyhound or two by their side.

Greyhound racing started at around the turn of the century with the invention of a lure coursing device that a dog could chase around an oval track. It quickly became popular in the US and Great Britain.

Retired racing greyhounds are calm couch potatoes and make a good choice for many families. There are many organizations that adopt retired dogs to suitable homes. Racing is in decline in the US, with only 4 states allowing it, but it's still active in the UK.

<u>**Colors**</u>

Any color or combination of colors is acceptable.

<u>**By the Numbers**</u>

AKC Breed Ranking: 142 out of 197 (2021)

Life expectancy: 10 to 13 years.

Size: 28 to 30 inches (male); 27 to 28 inches (female); weight: 65 to 70 lbs. (male), 60 to 65 lbs. (female).

Coat Care: 2 – low; Greyhounds enjoy a rub down, especially when shedding, but rarely need a bath.

Trainability: 4 – low; Greyhounds know what they want. If it's not what you want, it can be a challenge to bring them around to your way of thinking. The good news is that Greyhounds are naturally sweet tempered, quiet and clean, so going along with what they want is not usually that hard.

Energy Level: 5 – medium; they are generally elegant couch potatoes unless they see something to hunt. Then they are a 10 in energy and should never be let off leash in an open area.

Good with Children: 6 – medium; they enjoy children but prefer to watch their antics from the sidelines.

Noise Level: 2 – low; Greyhounds rarely bark.

Shedding Level: 5 – medium; Greyhounds shed seasonally.

Greyhound

"You can say any foolish thing to a dog, and the dog will give you a look that says, 'Wow, you are right! I never would have thought of that!'"

— Dave Berry

Harrier

Intelligent, Independent, Social

Harriers look like a giant Beagle or the English Foxhound's little brother, but really, they are their own ancient breed.

Friendly like a Beagle and hardworking like a Foxhound, this breed's specialty is not chasing the fox, but the hare.

His beautiful voice will bring tears to the eyes of hunting aficionados. But the neighbors will have a dim view of a bored Harrier's enthusiastic barking.

While their smaller cousin, the Beagle can be followed on foot, a Harrier is followed on horseback. If not actively hunting, the Harrier can excel as a runner's companion. But this independent breed is not a dog for an inexperienced owner. As a pack animal, he enjoys the company of other dogs.

History

As the dark ages waned, England's countryside slowly morphed from dense woods to rolling hills and farms. Aristocracy's need for hunting dogs morphed as well, from sturdy giant animals able to chase and take down the big British stag, to a medium sized dog capable of zigging and zagging over field and fence after another farmer's pest – the hare.

Dating back to the 1700's, the sport of Hound Trailing was created in Cumbria, in northern England. No animal was chased but a trail was laid down for the dogs to follow. The hound that finished first won.

The Harrier, being faster and more agile than the English Foxhound, has been the primary dog used in this sport. Hound Trailing has gained popularity, along with Harriers, as fox hunting was banned in the UK in 2004.

Colors

Harriers can be any color.

By the Numbers

AKC Breed Ranking: 190 out of 197 (2021)

Life expectancy: 12 to 15 years.

Size: 19 to 21 inches; weight: 45 to 60 lbs.

Coat Care: 4 – low; Harriers benefit from a good rub down every once in a while, and a bath if they get into the mud.

Trainability: 4 – low; they are amiable and willing but not very biddable. They do best in sports that showcase their native abilities.

Energy Level: 7 – medium; it's pretty logical that a breed bred to zig and zag, following a scent through field and stream is going to be high energy. But he is less energetic than the other scenting pack hounds; the Harrier is more a sprinter than a marathoner. If the breed gets plenty of walkies (or runs) and lots of ball chasing, the breed can make a friendly and successful family pet.

Good with Children: 8 – high; Harriers love kids, and kids love them.

Noise Level: 9 – high; the breed has a beautiful "bay", bred to let the huntsman know the scent is near. Of course, that big, beautiful bark can also inform in detail about the squirrels in the back yard, the full moon and the neighbors walking by. A bored Harrier is a noisy Harrier.

Shedding Level: 7 – medium; Harriers shed seasonally.

Harrier

"I have caught more ills from people sneezing over me and giving me virus infections than from kissing dogs."
— Barbara Woodhouse

Ibizan Hound

Springs for Legs

The Ibizan Hound could be what Superman had in mind when he said, "able to leap tall buildings in a single bound." This dog can jump higher than his own height from a standstill. Ibizans were bred to be able to work independently and hardy enough to chase down small game in the heat of the rocky hills on Ibiza, Majorca and the surrounding Balearic Islands. They hunt by sight, smell and hearing in packs of two or three. Coming down a rocky hill they can jump high over a bush, coming down on a rabbit mid-flight.

Because they are hard wired to be fabulous sprinters, Ibizan Hounds need plenty of exercise including a daily chance to really stretch out and run. It's no surprise they love lure coursing, but failing that, the chance to chase down a ball every day is critical. But because they hunt by many senses, they can be easily distracted – they are the original "Wow, is that a butterfly?!?" dog.

The breed has a hearty sense of humor and enjoys children. Beware if all is suddenly quiet in the room with your Ibizan and the kids – they are up to something.

Given enough exercise, Ibizan Hounds make mischievous and loyal companions.

History

3000 years ago, Phoenicians were the original traveling salesmen. Based in today's Lebanon, their territory was the countries bordering today's Europe. They brought the Egyptian coursing dogs to the Balearic Islands off the coast of Spain, where over time the breed developed into the Ibizan Hound.

Colors

White and red, in any combination.

By the Numbers

AKC Breed Ranking: 152 out of 197 (2021)

Life expectancy: 11 to 14 years.

Size: 23.5 to 27.5 inches (male); 22.5 to 26 inches (female); weight: 50 lbs. (male), 45 lbs. (female).

Coat Care: 2 – low; Ibizan Hounds enjoy a rub down, especially when shedding, but rarely need a bath.

Trainability: 5 – medium; Ibizan Hounds know what they want. If that's what you want, great. The trick in training them is to convince them that what you want is what they want. They can never be let off leash in the open, as if they see prey, they will take off.

Energy Level: 8 – high; this is a breed that can work long hours in harsh conditions. That's high energy. They need daily vigorous exercise, which can be chasing a ball, running with a human companion or taking long walks. They especially love lure coursing. When a Ibizan Hound gets enough exercise they can be mellow and happy family members.

Good with Children: 7 – medium; they enjoy children and make good buddies for adventures.

Noise Level: 2 – low; Ibizan Hounds rarely bark.

Shedding Level: 5 – medium; Ibizan Hounds shed seasonally.

Ibizan Hound

"Dogs lives are short, too short, but you know that going in. You know the pain is coming, you're going to lose a dog, and there is going to be great anguish, so you live fully in the moment with her, never fail to share her joy or delight in her innocence, because you can't support the illusion that a dog can be your lifelong companion. There's such beauty in the hard honesty of that, in accepting and giving love while always aware that it comes with an unbearable price."
— Dean Koontz

Irish Wolfhound

Huge, Intuitive, Athletic

The Irish Wolfhound is immense; strong enough to take on wolves or even the massive Irish elk (six ft. at the shoulder). The breed's motto is: "Gentle when stroked, fierce when provoked". This is a breed that tunes in to people's feelings. He can be bursting with energy, delicately precise, smart, engaging or comforting -- as needed.

History

The history of the Irish Wolfhound is quite literally the stuff of legend. There's Gelert, who was killed by his master's hand after saving his son from a wolf in a melancholy tale of mistake and remorse. Then there's Bran, the favorite of Irish Chieftain Fin Mac Coul.

The original blueprint of the Irish Wolfhound was created by mixing the indigenous large dogs of Britain with greyhounds brought in by those ultimate tradesmen, the Phoenicians. Fierce hunting dogs were described by Strabo in 24 AD as gigantic Greyhounds in use among the Pictish and Celtic nations. Hollinshed (16th century) said: "They are not without wolves, and greyhounds to hunt them, bigger of bone or limb than a colt".

Colors

Grey, Brindle, red, black, white or fawn.

<u>**By the Numbers**</u>

AKC Breed Ranking: 74 out of 197 (2021)

Life expectancy: 6 to 8 years.

Size: 32 inches (male), 30 inches (female); weight: 120 lbs. (male), 105 lbs. (female).

Coat Care: 6 – medium; regular brushing helps with tangles and shedding.

Trainability: 6 – medium; this is a naturally clean and sensible breed. The default of an Irish Wolfhound is to watch and relax. However, they will do what's necessary to have maximum hang time; if that includes learning new things, they are fine with that.

Energy Level: 6 – medium; they are a chill breed, as happy to lie in front of the fire as to go on a hike.

Good with Children: 7 – medium; they enjoy children of all ages and will follow their moods. They are also good with other dogs.

Noise Level: 2 – low; Irish Wolfhounds rarely bark. Why would they need to?

Shedding Level: 7 – medium; The breed does shed.

85

"Dogs are great. Bad dogs, if you really call them that,
are perhaps the greatest of them all."

— John Grogan

Norwegian Elkhound

Independent, Athletic, Brave, Friendly

Norwegian Elkhounds were bred to independently go after moose, a massive animal about 10 ft tall from hoof to antler, then hold them at bay until the hunter arrives. I wouldn't be thrilled to meet any wild creature twice as tall as myself. But the Elkhound is about 2 ft. tall, and he is cheerfully willing to take on a creature five times his height. That's brave.

This is a moderate, sturdy breed well able to do an honest day's work. Reserved with strangers, once properly introduced he makes a life-long friend. The breed is eager to learn as they enjoy anything where they can spend time with their people. They are fine with kids but shed profusely.

History

The Norwegian Elkhound is a member of the northern spitz breeds. Thousands of years ago, the Vikings needed dogs with outrageous courage to take on the big wild creatures like the moose (called "elg" in Norwegian) that threatened them. They used the local semi wild dogs, close cousins to the northern wolf, and selected carefully for the traits they were looking for. In the Viste Cave at Jaeren in Western Norway an Elkhound skeleton was found among the stone tools, dating from 4000 to 5000 BC. Among the many tales about the breed is one from the 1100s where an Elkhound was named king in the land of Throndhjem.

Colors

Norwegian Elkhounds are grey with black tips. There's black on his muzzle, ears and the tip of his tail.

By the Numbers

AKC Breed Ranking: 97 out of 197 (2021)

Life expectancy: 12 to 15 years.

Size: 20.5 inches (male), 19.5 inches (female); weight: 55 lbs. (male), 48 lbs. (female).

Coat Care: 5 – medium; Norwegian Elkhounds benefit from regular thorough brushing to keep his shedding under control.

Trainability: 7 – medium; while the breed is independent and brave enough to find and chase down a moose, they also have the typical northern spitz desire to hang out with their human buddies. They are down for any fun activity and do well in performance events.

Energy Level: 7 – medium; Norwegian Elkhounds are working dogs and have working dog energy. But if the breed gets plenty of walkies (or runs) and lots of ball chasing, the breed can make a friendly and successful family pet.

Good with Children: 7 – medium; Norwegian Elkhounds enjoy kids but at a certain point they can be done with them.

Noise Level: 9 – high; the breed was bred to hold a 10ft. high creature at bay with his bark, so it's logical that they can make noise with the best of them. Of course, that big, beautiful bark can also inform in detail about the squirrels in the back yard, the full moon and the neighbors walking by. A bored Norwegian Elkhound is a noisy Norwegian Elkhound.

Shedding Level: 9 – high; Norwegian Elkhounds shed copiously.

Norwegian

Elkhound

"Old dogs, like old shoes, are comfortable. They might be a bit out of shape and a little worn around the edges, but they fit well." — Bonnie Wilcox

Otterhound

Good-Natured, Exuberant, Shaggy

The Otterhound is the original shaggy dog. Bred to take on the otter, he is one of the few breeds with webbed feet and is an excellent swimmer. In the late Dark Ages, otters were so numerous in Great Britain that they threatened the livelihood of fishermen. Otterhounds were created to hunt them, but the breed did their job so well that they almost eliminated their prey, and otter hunting was outlawed in the UK in 1977.

Today Otterhounds are used to hunt raccoons, mink, bear, and mountain lion. They also make sturdy and friendly search and rescue dogs. They excel at any activity that uses their extraordinary sense of smell.

As their coat repels water, the Otterhound has a unique and powerful doggy odor. The breed is not hypoallergenic and does shed. They are slow to mature, mentally and physically but Otterhound lovers will tell you that they are worth the wait.

They get along well with kids and are always up for the next adventure.

History

We think of otters today as delightful and funny, the clowns of our estuaries and rivers.
But they are also prodigious seafood eaters. In the past otters had few predators, and there were a lot of them. Fisherman of the past – we are talking about 800 AD -- didn't think it was funny that otters were eating their livelihood, and they wanted something done about it.

Enter the Otterhound, a breed with an extraordinary nose, specifically bred to hunt in or out of the water. It looks like the origins of the Otterhound came from French hounds, as the breed bears a striking resemblance to the Grand Griffon Vendeen.

Colors

Any color or combination of colors.

By the Numbers

AKC Breed Ranking: 176 out of 197 (2021)

Life expectancy: 10 to 13 years.

Size: 24 to 27 inches (male), 23 to 26 inches (female); weight: 75 to 115 lbs. (male), 65 to 100 lbs. (female).

Coat Care: 6 – medium; regular brushing helps keep the burrs out and the tangles tamed.

Trainability: 7 – medium; Otterhounds are one of the more trainable hounds, especially for scenting and trailing activities.

Energy Level: 8 – high; they're a playful breed and enjoy nothing more than romping with their people or other dogs.

Good with Children: 8 – high; they enjoy children of all ages and are down for any mischief the kids might dream up.

Noise Level: 7 – medium; the breed is a good watchdog and will let you know what's going on; their booming bark is intimidating. They make a poor guard dog however as they love everyone, even the burglar come to pick up your silver.

Shedding Level: 7 – medium; Otterhounds shed.

Otterhound

93

"Anyone who doesn't know what soap tastes like,
never washed a dog." — Franklin Jones

Petit Bassett Griffon Vendeen

Friendly, Noisy, Energetic

The Petit Basset Griffon Vendeen is an energetic, scruffy clown who lives to play – until there is something to trail. Then he is all business. His rough wiry coat protects him from the briars and thorns of his native countryside – the coastal Vendeen, south of Brittany.

All puppies are darling, but this breed's babies are especially lovable – and that can be dangerous. If someone buys this puppy only because he looks sweet and adorable, they'll be disappointed; the puppy will grow up to be a high energy, noisy and friendly hunter. More kooky than cuddly and more intense than adorable.

The breed gets along well with family, kids and the neighbors. He's never met a stranger. He also enjoys hanging out with other dogs.

History

The creation of the Griffon Vendeen family started at least 400 years ago when French King Louis' Master of Hounds (called the "Greffier") crossed the Griffon de Bresse (a wheat-coated, rough-coated hound) with the royal white smooth coated hunting dogs. The smallest Griffon breeds thus created were the Petit Basset Griffon Vendeen. He was Basset (low to the ground) and moved slower, so people could follow him on foot.

The Petit Basset Griffon Vendeen was bred to hunt rabbit.

Colors

PBGVs are mostly white with any other color, and black and tan.

By the Numbers

AKC Breed Ranking: 164 out of 197 (2021)

Life expectancy: 13 to 15 years.

Size: 15.5 to 18 inches; weight: 40 to 45 lbs.

Coat Care: 5 – medium; regular brushing helps keep the burrs out and the tangles tamed.

Trainability: 6 – medium; Petit Basset Griffon Vendeens enjoy learning if it has to do with hunting or trailing by scent. They have a short attention span.

Energy Level: 8 – high; they're a playful breed and enjoy nothing more than romping with their people. An expert called living with PBGVs like being a member of "a circus of flying monkeys" – always busy and very inquisitive.

Good with Children: 8 – high; they enjoy children of all ages and are down with any mischief the kids might dream up.

Noise Level: 8 – medium; the breed is a good watchdog and will let you know what's going on. Sometimes you'll want to hear all about the latest, sometimes, not so much.

Shedding Level: 5 – medium; Petit Basset Griffon Vendeens do shed.

Petit Basset Griffon Vendeen

"I have found that when you are deeply troubled, there are things you can get from the silent devoted companionship of a dog that you can get from no other source." — Doris Day

Pharaoh Hound

Mischievous Clown, Escape Artist, Noble

The Pharaoh Hound is one of the few breeds that can blush. "His face glows like a god," wrote an admirer 3000 years ago. Like many of his cousin coursing breeds, he is strikingly elegant.

Pharaohs were bred to be able to work independently and hardy enough to chase down small game in the heat of the rocky hills on Malta, an island off the coast of Sicily.

Because they are hard wired to be fabulous sprinters, Pharaoh Hounds need plenty of exercise including a daily chance to really stretch out and run. It's no surprise they love lure coursing, but failing that, the chance to chase down a ball every day is critical.

As a sight hunter the Pharaoh Hound does not mesh well with small mammals like gerbils or rabbits; their quick movements can waken the Pharaoh Hound hunting instincts. The breed enjoys children, as they have a childlike sense of humor. Beware if all is suddenly quiet in the room with your Pharaoh and your kids – they are up to something.

Given enough exercise, Pharaoh Hounds make gentle and loyal companions.

History

3000 years ago, the Phoenicians were the original "have I got a deal for you" guys. Based in today's Lebanon, their sales territory were the countries bordering the Mediterranean and today's England. They brought the Egyptian coursing dogs to Malta, where over time the breed developed into the Pharaoh Hound.

Colors

Can range from a deep chestnut to a golden tan.

By the Numbers

AKC Breed Ranking: 172 out of 197 (2021)

Life expectancy: 12 to 14 years.

Size: 23 to 25 inches (male); 21 to 24 inches (female); weight: 45 to 55 lbs. (male).

Coat Care: 2 – low; Pharaoh Hounds enjoy a rub down, especially when shedding, but rarely need a bath.

Trainability: 5 – medium; Pharaoh Hounds know what they want. If that's what you want, great. The trick in training them is to convince them that what you want is what they want. They can never be let off leash in the open, as if they see prey they will take off.

Energy Level: 8 – high; this is a breed that can work long hours in harsh conditions. That's high energy. They need daily vigorous exercise, which can be chasing a ball, running with a human companion or taking long walks. They especially love lure coursing. When a Pharaoh Hound gets enough exercise they can be mellow and happy family members.

Good with Children: 6 – medium; they enjoy calm children and make good buddies for adventures with them. They are wary of strangers and need time to get used to new people.

Noise Level: 2 – low; Pharaoh Hounds rarely bark.

Shedding Level: 5 – medium; Pharaoh Hounds shed seasonally.

Pharaoh Hound

"Once you have had a wonderful dog, a life without one, is a life diminished." — Dean Koontz

The Sporting Dog of the Hound Group

The Plott Hound is the only coonhound without English Foxhound, Bloodhound, or French hound blood. He doesn't have that melty "houndy" look, and his ears do not come to his nose. Most are various shades of brindle which is also unique among coonhounds.

This breed can not only take on raccoons but also bear and wild boar. While many coonhounds look sweet and even cuddly, you'd never make that mistake with a Plott. Their look is determined and even intimidating.

Plotts aren't thrilled about strangers but are devoted to their people. They play well with other dogs and enjoy kids. But they live to hunt, or at the least, trail, and should have the opportunity to do so no matter what type of household they live in.

The breed is not hypoallergenic and special care needs to be taken of his ears to keep them free of infection.

History

The wily raccoon, plentiful in Southern and Midwest woods, provided both meat and fur to American pioneers. Coons were a pest, opening barn doors with sensitive paws and creating havoc within. But they were fast and clever and easily evaded the usual hunting dogs. If cornered, the coons climbed a tree and got away.

John Plott brought his 5 big dogs to North Carolina when he emigrated from Germany in the mid-1800s. It is thought that they were Hannover Hounds, a breed that was being used at the same time in the home country to help create the German Shorthaired Pointer. John and his brother Von collaborated with a local landowner named Hildebrand to create the Plott Hound.

Colors

Any shade of brindle is preferred. Black or buckskin is also accepted.

By the Numbers

AKC Breed Ranking: 167 out of 197 (2021)

Life expectancy: 11 to 12 years.

Size: 20 to 25 inches (male); 20 to 23 inches (female); weight: 50 to 60 lbs. (male), 40 to 55 lbs. (female).

Coat Care: 4 – low; Plott Hounds benefit from a good brushing to keep the shedding under control. They need a bath if they manage to get themselves covered with mud, and special and regular attention needs to be paid to their ears.

Trainability: 7 – medium; Plotts want to do right by their people. They are open to training in non-tracking pursuits. But they are still devoted hunters – they should always have an opportunity to fuel their passion to bring home game or trail.

Energy Level: 8 – high; they require plenty of exercise but adore playing with their people and other dogs.

Good with Children: 8 – high; they enjoy children and can tolerate kid shenanigans.

Noise Level: 8 – high; when Plott Hounds let loose it's a loud and ringing bay. If lonely or bored, they will serenade the neighborhood.

Shedding Level: 6 - medium: Plotts do sh ed.

Plott Hound

105

"A dog is one of the remaining reasons why some people can be persuaded to go for a walk."
— Orlando Aloysis Batista

Humorous, Independent, Cheeky

It's easy to think of the Portuguese Podengo Pequeno as a cute little companion, and they are all that. But you have to know that the breed is the smallest hunting dog, with a high energy level. They will take off to the next county if they smell something good. They need a job but it doesn't have to be hunting, just as good is being a kid buddy. They have a definite sense of humor but may think that things are funny that you don't. So beware!

The breed is not hypoallergenic and does shed.

History

The breed is the smallest of the Podengos – the other sizes are Medio (16 – 22 inches) and Grande (22 to 28 inches). They are one of the ten national dogs of Portugal. The ever-present Phoenician traders brought them to the Iberian shores about 3000 years ago. Podengo artifacts were discovered under the Lisbon Cathedral.

Colors

White with patches of yellow or fawn preferred. Black or brown, white with patches of black or brown are also acceptable.

<u>**By the Numbers**</u>

AKC Breed Ranking: 167 out of 197 (2021)

Life expectancy: 12 to 15 years.

Size: 8 to 12 inches; weight: 9 to 13 lbs.

 Coat Care: 4 – low; Portuguese Podengo Pequenos have two coat varieties, smooth, which is short and very dense, and wire, which is 1 to 3" and not as dense. The short coat Podengo needs an occasional rub down and bath, the wire benefits from a weekly brushing to take out the burrs and keep down any tangles.

Trainability: 7 – medium; Portuguese Podengo Pequenos, are a primitive breed (think not mixed with other breeds, same temperament for thousands of years) and love hunting above all else. But they also enjoy spending time with their people. If you can convince a Podengo that the training will allow them to spend more time with you, they'll be happy to do it.

Energy Level: 8 – high; they're a playful breed and enjoy nothing more than romping with their people or other dogs.

Good with Children: 8 – high; they enjoy children of all ages and are down with any mischief the kids might dream up.

Noise Level: 7 – medium; the breed is a good watchdog and will let you know what's going on. They are a bit wary of strangers.

Shedding Level: 7 – medium; Podengo Pequenos do shed.

Portuguese Podengo Pequeno

"A well-trained dog will make no attempt to share your lunch. He will just make you feel so guilty that you cannot enjoy it." — Helen Thomson

Pleading Expression, Comes to Life

when Game is Present

The Redbone Coonhound has matinee idol looks in a family of good old boys. It's all in the coat; the term "mahogany" does not do it justice – the color, to be accurate, should be called "lights up from within, warm your hands in it deep brown-red gold".

Redbones have the same Coonhound temperament of their fellow breeds; mellow and easy going at home, tireless and persistent on the trail of a racoon, with one addition: when you look into their eyes, you melt. So protect your lunch from them!

The Redbone Coonhound is not hypoallergenic and special care needs to be taken of his velvety ears to keep them free of infection.

History

Coonhounds were created to satisfy the American pioneers' need for food and warm coats. The wily raccoon, plentiful in Southern and Midwest woods, provided both meat and fur. And besides, coons were a pest, opening barn doors with sensitive paws and creating havoc within. But they were fast and clever and easily evaded the usual hounds. If cornered, the coons climbed a tree and got away. To create a dog that could hunt down a coon, English hounds brought over by Virginian plantation owners were bred with French hounds brought over by the Marquis de Lafayette and Bloodhounds; then breeders selected hardy, tenacious dogs that could a chase a coon up a tree and then keep the animal cornered until the hunters caught up.

The Redbone descends from red foxhounds brought to America by Scottish immigrants in the late 1700's (think Jamie and Claire Fraser of "Outlander"….) and Red Irish Foxhounds imported before the Civil War.

Colors

Solid red preferred. Dark muzzle and small amount of white on brisket and feet permissible.

By the Numbers

AKC Breed Ranking: 146 out of 197 (2021)

Life expectancy: 11 to 12 years.

Size: 22 to 27 inches (male); 21 to 26 inches (female); weight: 45 to 70 lbs.

Coat Care: 4 – low; Redbone Coonhounds benefit from a good brushing to keep the seasonal shedding under control. They need a bath if they manage to get themselves covered with mud, and special and regular attention needs to be paid to their ears.

Trainability: 7 – medium; Redbones are the most eager to please Coonhound. They are open to training in non-tracking pursuits as they are good with any sport that allows them to hang with their people. But they are still devoted hunters and should never be let off leash in open areas.

Energy Level: 8 – high; they require plenty of exercise but adore playing with their people and other dogs.

Good with Children: 8 – high; they enjoy children and can tolerate kid shenanigans.

Noise Level: 7 – medium; Redbone Coonhounds don't bark a lot. But when they do let loose it's a loud and ringing bay. Redbones love to be with their people or their buddy dogs – if they are left alone and lonely in the backyard they will broadcast their pain to the neighborhood.

Shedding Level: 7 – medium; Redbone Coonhounds shed seasonally.

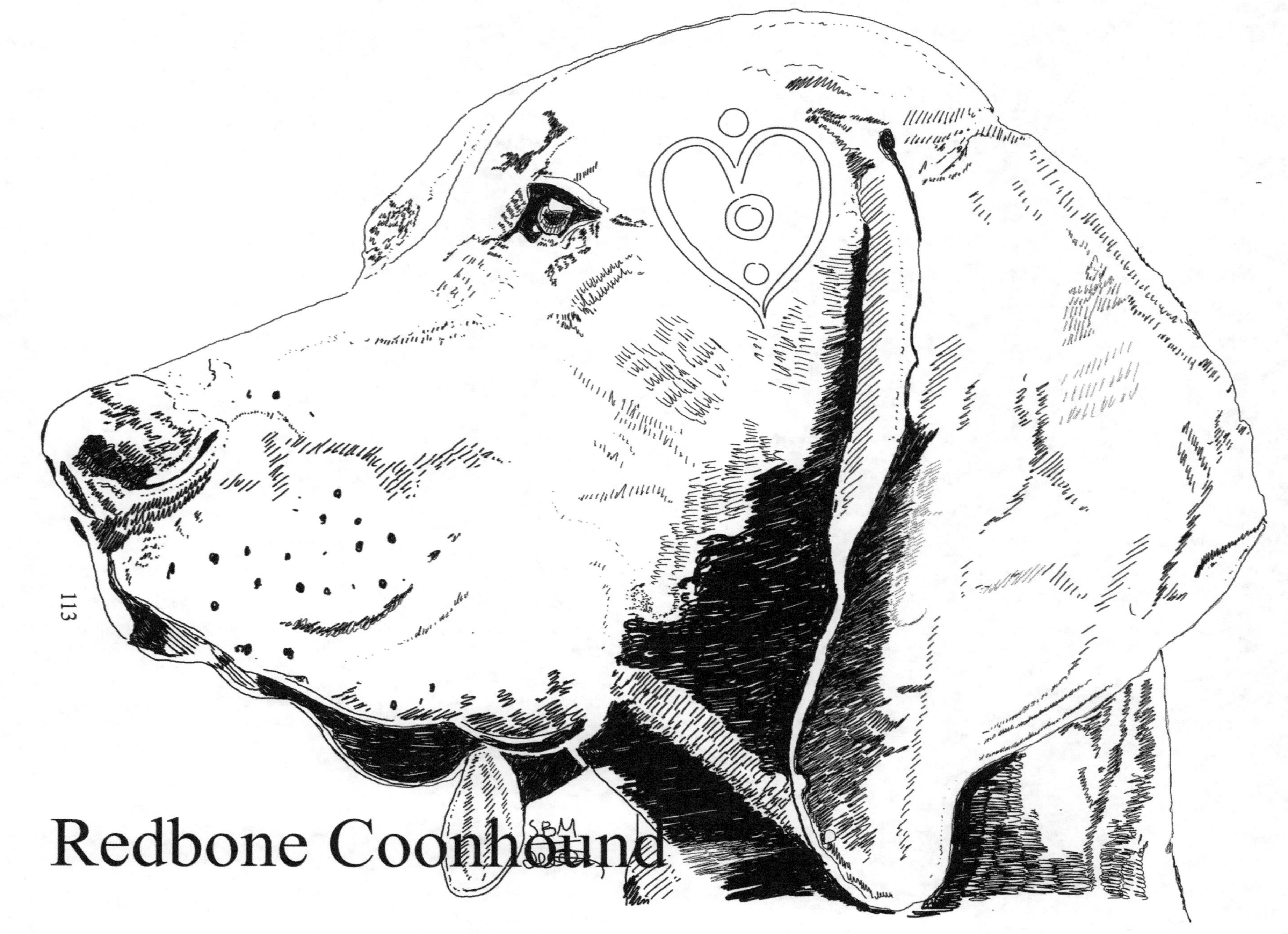

Redbone Coonhound

"In order to really enjoy a dog, one doesn't merely try to train him to be semi human. The point of it is to open oneself to the possibility of becoming partly a dog." — Edward Hoagland

Rhodesian Ridgeback

Loyal, Regal, Versatile

The Rhodesian Ridgeback is an all-purpose dog. Big and courageous enough to hold a lion at bay, with enough speed and stamina to keep up with the horses all day long and able to bring down a springbok or two along the way for the family pot, the Ridgeback defies categorization.

In the end, it matters less what to call him than to enjoy the breed in all its diversity.

The breed is not hypoallergenic and special care needs to be taken of his ears to keep them free of infection.

This is a working breed that needs a job. With enough things to do, the Ridgeback can make a delightful family pet.

History

350 years ago, the arriving Dutch settlers in w h a t is now South A frica needed a versatile dog that would

help th em ta me th e empty veldt. Plentiful in wild animals, the only otheople were hunter-gatherers called Bushmen, a small, peace-loving people with a language full of clicks. (The fierce Zulu arrived about 100 years later.) However, dogs brought by the Europeans quickly succumbed to the various African diseases.

Undeterred, the clever "Afrikaners" bred their European dogs with the Bushmans' "Hottentot" dogs, who were resistant to local disease. After time and a lot of experimentation, the result was the Rhodesian Ridgeback – a hardy, healthy breed, courageous enough to protect the farms from marauding big cats and with good enough scenting and sight hunting abilities to hunt for the pot. They had a mile-eating trot, able to keep up with horses as the farmers inspected their land.

The Hottentot dogs had a ridge (that is the hair grew in the opposite direction) down their back – the new breed had that as well.

Colors

All different shades of wheaten, so that the Rhodesian Ridgeback can blend into the African veldt.

By the Numbers

AKC Breed Ranking: 42 out of 197 (2021)

Life expectancy: 11 to 12 years.

Size: 25 to 27 inches (male); 24 to 26 inches (female); weight: 85 lbs. (male), 70 lbs. (female).

Coat Care: 4 – low; Rhodesian Ridgebacks benefit from a good rubdown to keep the shedding under control. They need a bath if they manage to get themselves covered with mud, and special and regular attention needs to be paid to their ears.

Trainability: 8 – high; Rhodesian Ridgebacks love to do anything that allows them to hang with their people. As a multi-purpose dog they have many interests, so can excel in many areas of tracking, confirmation, obedience, and performance.

Energy Level: 8 – high; they require plenty of exercise but adore playing with their people and other dogs.

Good with Children: 8 – high; they enjoy children and can tolerate kid shenanigans. They love going on adventures with the kids.

Noise Level: 4 – low; Rhodesian Ridgebacks have lots of other skill sets so don't need to bark to intimidate.

Shedding Level: 6 - medium; th e breed does sh ed

Rhodesian Ridgeback

"Dogs are our link to paradise. They don't know evil or jealousy or discontent. To sit with a dog on a glorious afternoon is to be back in Eden, where doing nothing was not boring – it was peace." – Milan Kundera

Saluki

Clever, Independent, Gentle

The Noble One

Elegant, Loyal, Very Fast

The Saluki is one of the breeds that you can look at floating along next to his elegant mistress in Manhattan and think "fashion accessory". But nothing could be further from the truth.

While a Saluki dearly loves spending time with his people, this is a primitive breed, hard-wired to be a most excellent hunter.

Given enough exercise, the breed makes a loyal and sweet companion. They are usually wary of strangers. The Saluki is perhaps the oldest of dog breeds; there's evidence of them as much as 7000 years ago.

If you want to own a piece of living history, a Saluki may be right for you.

History

Salukis were a favorite of kings; their ability to sight game was superb and their capacity to hunt tirelessly over harsh terrain was legendary. The Saluki's bodies were often mummified along with their pharaohs. There are several different styles of the breed, ranging from the heavier boned and heavier coated dogs originating in today's Iran to the smaller, racier dogs originating from the Sinai or Egypt.

Colors

White, cream, fawn, golden, red, grizzle and tan, tricolor (white, black and tan) and black and tan.

By the Numbers

AKC Breed Ranking: 120 out of 197 (2021)

Life expectancy: 10 to 17 years.

Size: 23 to 28 inches (male); considerably smaller (female); weight: 40 to 65 lbs.

Coat Care: 2 – low; Salukis enjoy a good brushing to tease the burs out of their fringes but rarely need a bath.

Trainability: 5 – medium; The Saluki is a primitive breed that knows what he wants. If that's what you want, great. It's good that they are natively clean, mellow dogs but it can be hard to get them to change their mind if needed. This is also a "watching" breed prone to striking a pose, or so it seems. (What they are really doing is spying that tuna sandwich left unattended at the other end of the house and calculating how to get it.)

Energy Level: 8 – high; while this is a breed that will work for hours in harsh conditions, they have a definite off switch and, given enough exercise, are happy to be homebodies as well. Vigorous exercise can be chasing a ball, running with a human companion, or taking long walks. They especially love lure coursing.

Good with Children: 6 – medium; they enjoy calm older children.

Noise Level: 2 – low; Salukis rarely bark.

Shedding Level: 5 – medium; Salukis shed infrequently, but they do shed.

Saluki

"Did you know that there are over 300 words for love
in canine?" — Gabriel Zezinho

Scottish Deerhound

Rugged Elegance, Dignified Good Humor

The Scottish Deerhound is a big hound, friendly without being effusive. You would think that his size would make him intimidating but that's not so. He has an inherent elegance that shines through. The breed has a gentle, dry sense of humor, more Bill Nighy ("About Time") than Rowan Atkinson (Mr. Bean). Above all else, he likes to spend time with his people and worries if family members don't get along.

The breed comes alive when chasing something and excels at sports such as lure coursing. He needs regular, vigorous exercise to stay healthy.

History

Evidence suggests that there were Deerhounds in what is now Scotland before the Scots got there in the 9th century. Massive, shaggy hounds were used by clan chieftains to take down the 400 lb. Scottish red deer with their punishing antlers. Greyhounds came into the mix at some point, producing the iconic reverse "S" of the greyhound type.

Colors

Dark blue-grey is most preferred. Next come the darker and lighter greys or brindles, the darker the better. Yellow and sandy red, red fawn especially with black ears and muzzles.

By the Numbers

AKC Breed Ranking: 166 out of 197 (2021)

Life expectancy: 8 to 11 years.

Size: 30 to 32 inches (male), 28 inches and up (female); weight: 85 to 110 lbs. (male), 75 to 95 lbs. (female).

Coat Care: 6 – medium; regular brushing helps with any shedding.

Trainability: 7 – medium; this is a naturally clean and sensible breed. The default of a Scottish Deerhound is to watch and relax. They are willing to do activities that their people enjoy, but they come alive when there is something to chase. They love lure coursing.

Energy Level: 7 – medium; they are a chill breed. While they are happy to lie all day in front of the fire, for optimum health they need daily vigorous exercise.

Good with Children: 7 – medium; they enjoy children of all ages but their specialty is to be a most excellent companion of older kids. They are also good with other dogs.

Noise Level: 2 – low; Scottish Deerhounds rarely bark. Why would they need to?

Shedding Level: 7 – medium; The breed does shed.

Scottish Deerhound.

"I sometimes look into the face of my dog Stan and see
a wistful sadness and existential angst, when all he is
actually doing is slowly scanning the ceiling for flies."
— Merrill Markoe

Powerful, Noble, Devoted, Graceful

When looking at a Sloughi, it should be obvious that the dog is a cut, athletic dog fully capable of working all day in harsh, sweltering conditions.

Known as the "Arabian Greyhound", the breed was a valuable partner with the Berbers and Bedouins of North Africa, being an excellent sight and scent hunter of everything from rabbits to gazelles.

Given enough exercise, Sloughis make loyal and sweet companions. They are usually wary of strangers.

Their big dark eyes speak of melancholy, but beware; your dog might just be thinking about that last piece of your sandwich!

History

Sloughi are one of those primitive breeds whose origins are at least 5000 years old. The Sloughi developed in North Africa, the Azawakh in the South Sahara and the Saluki in the Middle East. All three breeds were developed to course game across the vast and varied Sahara.

Berber cavalrymen who accompanied Hannibal across the Alps could easily have introduced the Sloughi to Europe.

Colors

All shades of light sand, through red fawn to mahogany, with or without brindling or black markings such a a black mask or black ears. Small to medium white marks are allowed.

By the Numbers

AKC Breed Ranking: 192 out of 197 (2021)

Life expectancy: 11 to 14 years.

Size: 26 to 29 inches (male); 24 to 27 inches (female); weight: 45 to 70 lbs.

Coat Care: 2 – low; Sloughis enjoy a rub down, especially when shedding, but rarely need a bath.

Trainability: 6 – medium; The Sloughi is a primitive breed that knows what he wants. If that's what you want, great. It's good that they are natively clean, mellow dogs but it can be hard to get them to change their mind if necessary. They excel at lure coursing.

Energy Level: 7 – medium; while this is a breed that will work for hours in harsh conditions, they have a definite off switch and, given enough exercise, are happy to be home bodies as well. Vigorous exercise can be chasing a ball, running with a human companion or taking long walks.

Good with Children: 7 – medium; they enjoy calm older children and make excellent companions for them.

Noise Level: 2 – low; Sloughis rarely bark.

Shedding Level: 4 – low; Sloughis shed infrequently, but they do shed.

Sloughi

"If I could be half the human my dog is, I'd be twice the human I am."

— Charles Yu

Treeing Walker Coonhound

Go Yonder, Get Deep, Get Treed Type of Coonhound

The Treeing Walker Coonhound is called "the People's Choice" as he simply knows how to get the job done. The Treeing Walker has the same Coonhound temperament as his fellow breeds; mellow and easy going at home, tireless and persistent on the trail of a racoon. Kept in a non-hunting home, a Treeing Walker needs a regular outlet for his energy.

The Treeing Walker Coonhound is not hypoallergenic and special care needs to be taken of his velvety ears to keep them free of infection.

<u>History</u>

Coonhounds were created to satisfy the American pioneers' need for food and warm coats. The wily raccoon, plentiful in Southern and Midwest woods, provided both meat and fur. And besides, coons were a pest, opening barn doors with sensitive paws and creating havoc within. But they were fast and clever and easily evaded the usual hounds. If cornered, the coons climbed a tree and got away. To create a dog that could hunt down a raccoon, English hounds brought over by Virginian plantation owners were bred with French hounds brought over by the Marquis de Lafayette and Bloodhounds; then breeders selected hardy, tenacious dogs that could a chase a coon up a tree and then keep the animal cornered until the hunters caught up.

The Treeing Walker descends from the Walker Foxhound, which evolved from English Foxhounds brought over by the Virginia plantation owners. It is a fast "hot nosed" hound (which means they prefer a fresh trail) and they range farther out than their fellow Coonhounds. Good that they have a ringing voice to let the hunter know where they are!

Colors

Tricolor of black, white and tan preferred.

By the Numbers

AKC Breed Ranking: 153 out of 197 (2021)

Life expectancy: 12 to 13 years.

Size: 22 to 27 inches (male); 20 to 25 inches (female); weight: 50 to 70 lbs.

Coat Care: 4 – low; Treeing Walker Coonhounds benefit from a good brushing to keep the seasonal shedding under control. They need a bath if they manage to get themselves covered with mud, and special and regular attention needs to be paid to their ears.

Trainability: 6 – medium; Treeing Walkers are eager hunters and love any training related to it.

Energy Level: 8 – high; they require plenty of exercise but adore playing with their people and other dogs.

Good with Children: 8 – high; they enjoy children and are a mellow buddy with them.

Noise Level: 7 – medium; Treeing Walker Coonhounds don't bark a lot. But when they do voice their opinion, it's loud and ringing. This is not a breed to leave alone for hours in the backyard, as they will sing their loneliness to the neighborhood.

Shedding Level: 7 – medium; Treeing Walker Coonhounds shed seasonally.

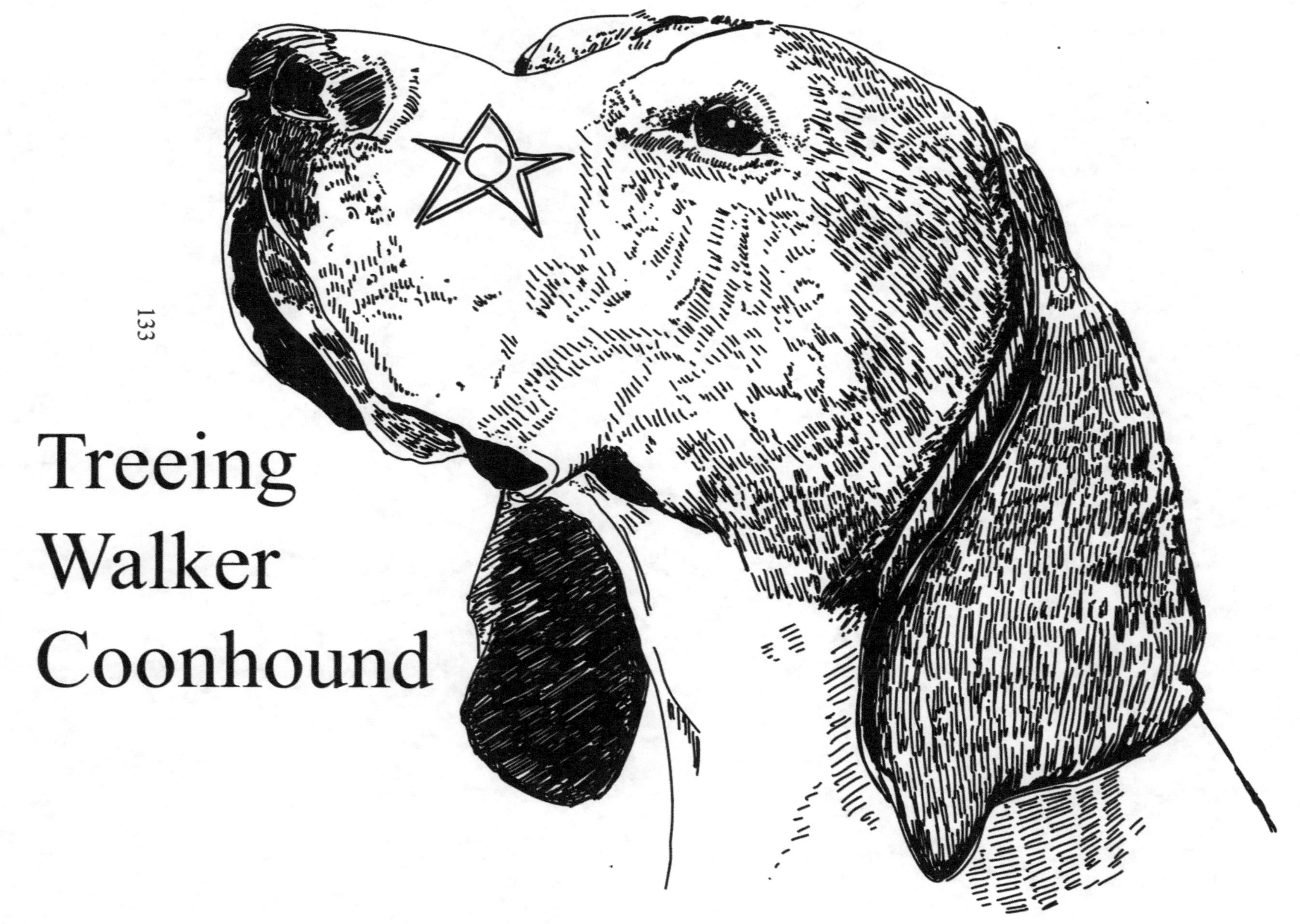

Treeing
Walker
Coonhound

"You know a dog can snap you out of any kind of mood you are in faster than you can think of." — Jill Abramson

Whippet

Fast, Elegant, Loyal, Mischievous

The Whippet is the fastest dog out there for his size; the breed can sprint up to 35 mph. Compare that to the fastest human (Usain Bolt) whose record is 27.8 mph.

You would think that such a fast animal would be hyper and nervous but nothing is further from the truth. Whippets are generally laid-back loungers, but they do love to play, either with humans or other dogs. They can get into mischief when hanging out with their own kind just like kids; and as any mother will tell you if the kids are suddenly quiet, you better go and check out what's going on.

Because they are hard wired to be fabulous sprinters, Whippets need plenty of exercise including the chance to really stretch out and run. It's no surprise they love lure coursing, but failing that, the chance to chase down a ball every day is critical.

As a sight hunter the Whippet does not mesh well with small mammals like gerbils or rabbits; their quick movements can waken the Whippet's hunting instincts. The breed enjoys children in moderation – they don't tolerate kid shenanigans well.

History

It has to be obvious that the Greyhound is the major ancestor of the Whippet. British north county coal miners enjoyed dog racing, but they didn't have the funds to pay for or the room to house Greyhounds. Rather than shrug their shoulders, they came up with a practical solution: breed a smaller dog. To the basic Greyhound blueprint, the clever miners mixed in local terriers and Italian Greyhounds. Called "the Poor Man's Racehorse" and the "Lightening Rag Dog" the new breed was expert at chasing a rag on a straight course, which was an early version of lure coursing.

At the turn of the last century, Lancaster textile workers emigrated in numbers to the busy mill towns of New England, bringing along their Whippets. They also brought their enthusiasm for Whippet racing, which has remained popular to this day.

<u>**Colors**</u>

Any color or combination of colors is acceptable.

<u>**By the Numbers**</u>

AKC Breed Ranking: 59 out of 197 (2021)

Life expectancy: 12 to 15 years.

Size: 19 to 22 inches (male); 18 to 21 inches (female); weight: 25 to 40 lbs.

Coat Care: 2 – low; Whippets enjoy a rub down, especially when shedding, but rarely need a bath.

Trainability: 6 – medium; Whippets know what they want. If it's not what you want, it can be a challenge to bring them around to your way of thinking. But they are more biddable than their big cousin the Greyhound.

Energy Level: 5 – medium; they are generally elegant couch potatoes. They enjoy the company of other dogs but can get into mischief when they are in a pack.

When they see something to chase, they are a 10 in energy and should never be let off leash in an open area.

Good with Children: 6 – medium; they enjoy children but need to be protected from a kid's wilder shenanigans.

Noise Level: 2 – low; Whippets rarely bark.

Shedding Level: 5 – medium; Whippets shed seasonally.

Whippet

137

What is a Responsible Breeder?

It's scary to purchase a puppy. With other products, you can check Yelp or Consumer Reports to see if a company is reputable. It's different with breeders. How do you tell in a few minutes whether the voice on the phone or the person at the other end of the emails is responsible?

Some people might think that it's someone who doesn't make any money from selling puppies. Or maybe it's someone who only has one female or someone who refuses to ship. None of those things are the gauge of a responsible breeder.

But there *are* some things to watch out for. Here's 11 indicators of a responsible breeder.

1. **She will want to know about you.** She will probably start out by inundating you with all sorts of questions about your home, your work, and your family. This is because she is trying to fit the correct dog to you. As a matter of fact, she will refuse to sell you a dog she doesn't honestly feel is right for you. If a breeder does not ask you at least as many questions as you ask her, she is not responsible.

2. **In Florida and most other states, a breeder is required to sell a dog with a Health Certificate, meaning that the puppy is vet certified as healthy, up to date on his shots and free of worms and fleas within the last 30 days.** A breeder that tries to sell you a puppy without a vet checked guarantee of heath at point of sale is not responsible.

3. **Listen to a breeder's stories about her adult dogs.** The breeder's purpose should be to create healthy adults that look and act like the breed. If she only talks about how cute her puppies are, she is often not a reputable breeder.

4. **She is willing for you to see her dogs in her home.** Sometimes the closest breeder for your chosen breed is thousands of miles away, so this is not feasible. But if you live nearby and your breeder keeps on making excuses about coming to her house, she is probably not responsible.

5. **A responsible breeder knows about her breed.** She can bend your ear for quite some time about its characteristics and history. She knows her breed's standard thorough and through and does everything in her power to follow it, though she recognizes that she will never be 100% successful. She is honest and forthright about the shortcomings of her breed as well as its sterling qualities. A breeder that says or implies that her breed is perfect in all circumstances is not reputable. And a breeder that refuses to follow certain parts of her standard and breeds odd colors or a different coat is absolutely not reputable.

6. **Most responsible breeders also show their dogs.** The purpose of dog shows is to sort out the best sires and dams for the next generation. Breeders should have enough pride in their stock to want to see how well they stack up against others.

7. **A responsible breeder regularly tests her breeding stock.** There can be genetic difficulties in

8. any line. Ignorance is not bliss. If a breeder doesn't regularly test her breeding stock, she is not reputable.

9. **A responsible breeder will work with you beyond the point of sale.** You should be able to call or email your breeder and get help at any point in the life of your dog. She knows that most training problems stem from you either working with your dog incorrectly or not responding quickly and appropriately to a problem. But rather than blame you, a responsible breeder helps you do it right.

10. **Most reputable breeders are willing to take back a dog that doesn't work out.** They don't want any of their dogs ending up at a shelter or leading a life of quiet misery because they can't fit into your family's lifestyle.

11. **A responsible breeder takes excellent care of her dogs.** This is far more important than how many dogs she has.

12. **Though the great majority of responsible breeders have bills far higher than their income, there is nothing wrong with a breeder making money.** She should sell her puppies for at least enough money to approach her expenses. Puppies that are far cheaper than normal often indicate a breeder that doesn't have pride in her stock.

I hope this helps you sort this out. Given the above points, you should be able to find someone who can become a real partner with you for the life of your dog. Good luck!

What Makes a Responsible Pet Owner?

My friend and I got on the subject the other day. She volunteers at an animal shelter. We were having coffee.

"I gotta tell you what happened."

"Right before closing, I had this lady at my counter with a small black dog.

'It's not my fault,' the lady told me. 'This dog is obviously over-bred. I was promised that he wouldn't shed, but he does – everywhere. And he pees everywhere too.

'The kids begged and begged for a dog. I gave in but I told them, you'll have to take care of him yourselves. And of course, they agreed. But did they? Of course not! It all got dumped on me. As usual. Never wanted the stupid thing in the first place.

'Last night I got up to get a drink of water and stepped straight into a big pile of dog poop. That was the final straw.

'I'm sure you understand I did all I could. The dog is obviously over-bred. It's not my fault!'

My friend gave a deep sigh. "The woman so floored me, I couldn't think of what to say. I came through the counter, took the dog's leash and led him away. He was a sweet little boy and no trouble at all. I took a long walk afterward.

"How can people get it so *wrong*?"

I shook my head. "No one ever tells people *how* to be a responsible pet owner. Instead, they get their ears and eyeballs filled up with stories of Evil Breeders. Victimhood is so much simpler than to stand up and take responsibility.

"It's way too easy to put a solitary bulls-eye on all breeders as the blanket cause of shelters full of abandoned animals. A good dog breeder is part of the solution, but so is a responsible pet *owner*.

"The popular press is curiously silent about this. It is loud about titillatingly horrific videos of stomach-turning breeding facilities, and we hear a lot these days about "over-bred" problem dogs.

"But what about the other side of the coin?"

I thought about our conversation over the next several days. What makes a responsible pet owner?

I figured there were ten things to watch out for.

1. **A responsible pet owner is not in a rush to get a dog.** She knows that she is purchasing a companion who will be with her for the next 15 years. She does not try to get a dog for under the Christmas tree or for a birthday.

2. **A responsible pet owner never gets a dog just "for the kids".** She knows that at least one adult household member must be willing to be fully responsible for the animal.

3. **Unless she is a responsible breeder, a responsible pet owner does not breed.** She never wants to "just have one litter" so the kids can see "the miracle of birth".

4. **A responsible pet owner realizes that even with busy modern lifestyles, dogs need exercise.** This is including regular walks. She knows that many canine behavior problems can be eliminated or at least mitigated with enough exercise.

5. **Whenever possible, she takes her dog with her.** She knows that a happy dog is one with lots of stimulation and interaction.

6. **A responsible pet owner microchips her dog and has him registered with one of the lost and found organizations.** She also has him licensed with her county.

7. **A responsible pet owner keeps up with her dog's health.** She checks him weekly for possible health issues and makes sure her dog gets regular wellness exams.

8. **A responsible pet owner trains her dog.** This can be informal classes out of a book if that's all that's available, but dogs love to learn; they become more sociable and excellent companions through training. If her dog has behavior problems, a responsible pet owner is persistent in looking for help and keeps going until she finds workable answers. She also realizes that if there is a persistent problem, most likely there is something that she is doing that is perpetuating the problem.

9. **A responsible pet owner continues to educate herself.** She keeps on learning about her breed, possible health issues and the latest in training protocols.

10. **A responsible pet owner knows that once she has made the original commitment, her dog is her responsibility for life.** Like a child or a marriage, there are no givebacks because the dog is no longer "convenient" or "entertaining". It's in sickness or in health, 'til death do us part.

I gave my friend the list. "What do you think?"

"I'm framing this and putting this on the wall behind the counter."

"That would be great. If it helps just one dog have a better, more responsible owner, it'll be worth it."

I've heard about the excellent responsible pet ownership program they have in Calgary, Canada. Maybe that's why that city has the lowest kill rate (how many pets are put to sleep) in North America.

Maybe this is one of the missing puzzle pieces in the problem of pets in shelters.

Just maybe.

Biography

My mother took me to my first dog show when I was eight. This fascinated me, and I immediately wanted to show our Standard Poodle.

Mom explained the many reasons why this wasn't possible, and I understood but there was a little voice in my head that said, "Someday you're going to do that." Of course, being eight, the next week I was telling everyone that I wanted to be a jockey.

I have always loved to draw and filled sketchbooks with an attempt at professionalism. My older sister Lucy was much better than me, so one day in frustration I asked her, "How do you get to be so good?"

"Draw what you see," she replied. It's the best art advice I've ever received. Following that tip, I have always created works that just seemed right to me – realistic, accurate but with a twinkle that no photograph could capture.

While living in Germany I was accepted as an art student by the Munich Academy. I attended one day of classes where I was told bluntly that I was doing everything wrong, that I needed to fix all my techniques and procedures. Hmm, I thought. Maybe I'll do just fine on my own. Never went back.

As a young mom, I started breeding and showing Silky Terriers. I loved it – it was the fulfillment of a dream. Fast forward almost 40 years and Tessier Silky Terriers has just completed its 130th AKC champion and we have had many top winners, including two World Champions. For more information about our dogs, you can visit www.tessier-silky-terriers.com.

Several years ago, it occurred to me that it would be fun to take up drawing again, this time specializing in canine art. As well as custom work, I have an ever-expanding line of greeting and special occasion cards, available at https://sandy-bergstrom-mesmer-designs.myshopify.com. I also have a line of over 150 pen and ink limited edition prints. In 2012 I won a Maxwell for my German Shepherd "Headshot" print. It can be seen on the German Shepherd breed page.

Both "Color Me Canine (Toy Group)" and "Color Me Canine (Herding Group)" have also won Maxwells.

Sandy Bergstrom Mesmer 2021
Sandy Bergstrom Mesmer Designs